WORKBOOK

ARCHITECTURE
RESIDENTIAL DRAFTING AND DESIGN

MW00990032

CLOIS E. KICKLIGHTER, CSIT

Dean Emeritus, School of Technology
and Professor Emeritus of Construction Technology
Indiana State University
Terre Haute, Indiana

JOAN C. KICKLIGHTER, CFCS
Coauthor of *Residential Housing*
Naples, Florida

Publisher
The Goodheart-Willcox Company, Inc.
Tinley Park, Illinois

Goodheart-Willcox Publisher Brand Disclaimer:
Brand names, company names, and illustrations for products and services included in this text are provided for educational purposes only, and do not represent or imply endorsement or recommendation by the author or the publisher.

The Goodheart-Willcox Company, Inc., Safety Notice: The reader is expressly advised to carefully read, understand, and apply all safety precautions and warnings described in this book or that might also be indicated in undertaking the activities and exercises described herein to minimize risk of personal injury or injury to others. Common sense and good judgment should also be exercised and applied to help avoid all potential hazards. The reader should always refer to the appropriate manufacturer's technical information, directions, and recommendations; then proceed with care to follow specific equipment operating instructions. The reader should understand these notices and cautions are not exhaustive.

The publisher makes no warranty or representation whatsoever, either expressed or implied, including but not limited to equipment, procedures, and applications described or referred to herein, their quality, performance, merchantability, or fitness for a particular purpose. The publisher assumes no responsibility for any changes, errors, or omissions in this book. The publisher specifically disclaims any liability whatsoever, including any direct, indirect, incidental, consequential, special, or exemplary damages resulting, in whole or in part, from the reader's use or reliance upon the information, instructions, procedures, warnings, cautions, applications or other matter contained in this book. The publisher assumes no responsibility for the activities of the reader.

Introduction

This workbook is designed for use with the text **Architecture—residential drafting and design**. The questions, problems, and activities are aimed at helping you master the subject matter included in the text. The many drawing problems guide you in developing a certain amount of skill in creating architecture designs and construction drawings in an accepted manner.

Each chapter in this workbook covers material in the corresponding chapter of the text. After studying a chapter in the text, try to complete as many questions as you can without referring to the text. Then, search out answers to the remaining questions. Study the examples and material in the text to work the problems.

The workbook includes several types of questions, problems, and activities. In some instances, you will be required to identify the parts shown in an illustration. Other activities require that you collect materials or prepare a notebook. Many tasks require that you complete a drawing or make a typical construction drawing. Several types of questions have been included: Multiple choice, matching, completion, short answer/listing, and calculations.

The workbook problems will require the use of the following architectural drawing equipment: Pencils; erasers; erasing shields; a T-square, straightedge, or drafting machine; triangles; protractors; an engineer's scale; an architect's scale; case instruments; irregular curves; pencil pointing devices; an assortment of 1/4 scale templates; and drafting tape. Most of the problems are to be completed on the pages of the workbook. Others, however, will require larger sheets that you must provide. Two standard sizes of tracing vellum—B-size (12″ × 18″) and C-size (18″ × 24″)—will be required. Drawings made with B-size and C-size sheets may be drawn in the traditional manner or with a CADD system. Several workbook-size sheets are included after the chapter material in the workbook for other problems designed by your instructor.

In addition to the problems presented in this workbook, the Architecture Software package is also available. It includes 89 problems, many of which are taken from the workbook. The problems selected for the package are the ones best suited for solutions completed with a CADD system. The Architecture Software package is not intended to replace the workbook, but rather facilitate the use of a CADD system in solving many of the workbook problems.

After studying each text chapter and successfully completing the workbook chapters, you will have developed a solid background in the design and drawing of residential structures. Further expertise can be developed through the design of more complex structures, further study of building codes, and research in material applications and building recommendations.

Clois E. Kicklighter

Joan C. Kicklighter

Contents

		Textbook Page	Workbook Page

The World of Architecture

1

Text, Pages 17–36

Name _____

Course _____ Date _____ Score _____

Part I: Matching

Match the correct house style with the characteristics listed below. Place the corresponding letter on the space provided.

A. Cape Ann   D. Garrison   G. Salt Box
B. Cape Cod   E. New England Gambrel   H. Southern Colonial
C. Contemporary   F. Ranch

1. The long, low roofline gently slopes from the ridge to the eaves to help combat bitter winter winds. The name of this house style is derived from containers used for food products.

1. _____

2. This house style has a large, centrally located chimney and a gambrel roof. The attic may be converted to living or sleeping space.

2. _____

3. A unique feature of this house style is the overhanging second story. This style also has a steep pitched roof and narrow siding.

3. _____

4. Ornate woodwork, iron trim, three-story chimneys, upper and lower balconies, front colonnades, and porticoes are some unique features of this elegant home style.

4. _____

5. The features of this popular house style include a gable roof with the top of the windows near the roofline, narrow siding, and shutters on the windows.

5. _____

6. A low-pitch roof with gables and overhanging eaves is characteristic of this one-story home style. Some homes have an "L" shape and an attached garage.

6. _____

7. This home style varies in design and use of materials. Some homes with this style borrow ideas from past designs while others are completely innovative. Plans are designed to please the homeowner.

7. _____

8. The name of this house style came from one of its features. It is found in most sections of the country. Two advantages of this style include usable space as a result of the roof design and shorter rafters.

8. _____

Part II: Completion

Complete each sentence with the proper response. Place your answer on the space provided.

1. Some homes are designed for particular settings such as a _____, seashore, or a steep cliff.

1. _____

2. The trends in architecture are to design homes to complement the site, _____, and retain privacy.

2. _____

3. _____ architectural design combines traditional and contemporary characteristics and is reminiscent of past styles.

3. _____

4. Modern materials and building techniques help homes to be _____ and weather-resistant.

4. _____

5. Older, structurally solid homes may be _____ to their original beauty.

5. _____

6. Under a cooperative, an apartment building is managed and run as a _____.

6. _____

7. The apartment and a share of the common ground are purchased, taxes are paid as though it were a separate house, and owners of units have joint interest in all the shared property and facilities. These are all characteristics of _____.

7. _____

8. The Americans with Disabilities Act (ADA) became law in _____.

8. _____

Part III: Short Answer/Listing

Provide brief answers to the following questions.

1. The distinguishing construction technique of the Garrison home has three advantages. What are they? _____

_____

_____

_____

2. List three trends in residential architecture that are prevalent today. _____

_____

_____

3. Name three types of multifamily housing structures. _____

_____

_____

Basic House Designs

2

Text, Pages 37–50

Name _____

Course _____ Date _____ Score _____

Part I: Multiple Choice
Select the best answer and write the corresponding letter in the space provided.

1. Which of the following is a feature of the one-story ranch design?

    A. Minimal heating costs.
    B. Economical to build.
    C. Easily adapted to indoor-outdoor living.
    D. Limited hall space.

    1. _____

2. Which of the following basic house designs is suitable for older or handicapped persons?

    A. One-story ranch.
    B. One-and-one-half-story.
    C. Two-story.
    D. Split-level.

    2. _____

3. Outside maintenance is generally easy on a one-story ranch design because:

    A. It has a small outside wall area.
    B. It has a low-pitched roof.
    C. It is built on a sloping lot.
    D. All of the above.

    3. _____

4. Dormers are usually added to this design to achieve more livable space.

    A. One-story ranch.
    B. One-and-one-half-story.
    C. Two-story.
    D. Split-level.

    4. _____

5. Advantages of the one-and-one-half-story design include:

    A. The attic may be expanded to achieve more livable space.
    B. Dormers may be added for light and ventilation.
    C. Heating costs are minimized.
    D. All of the above.

    5. _____

6. Which of the following best describes a two-story design?

    A. Little hall space is needed, and the sleeping, living, and service areas are on different levels.

    B. About one-third of the ceiling is directly under the roof, so adequate ventilation and insulation should be provided.

    C. It is economical to build, it requires a smaller lot, and it has a small roof and foundation area compared to the interior space of most other designs.

    D. It is built on one level. Thus, patios, porches, and terraces are possible outside any room.

6. _____

7. Advantages of the two-story design include:

    A. Heating is relatively simple and economical because heat naturally rises from the first to the second floor.

    B. The style is popular today because many variations on the basic design are possible.

    C. Exterior maintenance is simple and requires no special equipment.

    D. All of the above.

7. _____

8. This house design lends itself to easy cooling since the ceiling is not directly under the roof. Several windows provide effective ventilation.

    A. One-story ranch.
    B. One-and-one-half-story.
    C. Two-story.
    D. Split-level.

8. _____

9. Which of the following house designs takes advantage of a sloping or hilly lot?

    A. One-story ranch.
    B. One-and-one-half-story.
    C. Two-story.
    D. Split-level.

9. _____

10. The family room, garage, and foyer are commonly found on this level in a split-level design:

    A. Basement level.
    B. Intermediate level.
    C. Living level.
    D. Sleeping level.

10. _____

Name _____

11. Which of the following is a feature of the split-level design?

    A. It easily accommodates patios and terraces in the recreation area.
    B. The design makes efficient use of space.
    C. It may be built with either a basement or crawl space.
    D. All of the above.

11. _____

Part II: Short Answer/Listing

Provide brief answers to the following questions.

1. Without proper design and planning, heating may be a problem in a split-level design. What steps may be taken to solve the problem? _____

_____

_____

2. Name the three variations of the split-level design. _____

_____

_____

3. Which variation of the split-level design is most suitable for a lot that is high in front and low in back? _____

4. What is unique about the entry of a traditional split-level? _____

_____

_____

5. Traffic circulation should be planned for maximum efficiency. Explain why the foyer and garage play an important role in planning a house. _____

_____

_____

_____

6. Name the four basic house designs. _____

_____

_____

Primary Considerations

3

Text, Pages 51–65

Name _____

Course _____ Date _____ Score _____

Part I: Completion
Complete each sentence with the proper response. Place your answer on the space provided.

1. The house is the biggest item in terms of home investment. The _____ ranks second and should be evaluated carefully to realize its potential as a vital part of the home and its setting.

1. _____

2. A _____ home design is ideal for a hilly or sloping site.

2. _____

3. The structure should appear to be part of the _____.

3. _____

4. A competent attorney should examine the deed and _____ before the site is purchased.

4. _____

5. _____ ordinances determine whether commercial, multi-family, or single-family structures may be built on the intended site.

5. _____

6. The type of house that can be built on any given site is subject to local _____ codes.

6. _____

7. Information on permit costs, inspections, or regulations may be obtained from the local _____ inspector or local building department.

7. _____

8. The _____ is just as important as the size of the lot in determining construction possibilities.

8. _____

9. Family _____ is a major consideration in house design.

9. _____

10. The considerations in planning a residential structure include exterior design, size, and _____ as well as the ability to resell the house.

10. _____

11. A home designed around standard sizes called _____ results in less wasted material.

11. _____

12. The size of plywood and paneling is generally _____.

12. _____

13. Exterior walls should be modular lengths in multiples of 2′ or _____.

13. _____

14. Plan interior rooms around standard sizes of carpeting, which are available in widths of 12′ or _____.

14. _____

15. The _____ of living provided by the structure is a measure of the architect's success in solving a problem.

15. _____

Part II: Matching
Match the correct term with its description listed below. Place the corresponding letter on the space provided.

A. Building codes
B. Deed
C. Easements
D. Restrictions
E. Specifications
F. Title search
G. Topographical drawings

1. It determines if there are any legal claims against the property.

1. _____

2. This is a legal document through which ownership of the property is transferred.

2. _____

3. These may specify the style and size of the house that can be built on the property, as well as the type of landscaping and the overall cost of the house.

3. _____

4. These may allow utilities to cross the property or may prevent the filling in of a low area that must remain for drainage purposes.

4. _____

5. These involve plumbing, electrical, and building standards.

5. _____

6. These illustrate slope, contour, size, shape, elevation, trees, rocks, and soil conditions.

6. _____

7. These describe the quality of materials and workmanship.

7. _____

Part III: Multiple Choice
Select the best answer and write the corresponding letter in the space provided.

1. This plan locates switches, convenience outlets, ceiling outlet fixtures, and the panel box.

1. _____

A. Foundation plan.
B. Plumbing plan.
C. Plot plan.
D. Electrical plan.

2. These drawings include specifics of kitchens, stairs, chimneys, and fireplaces, and items of special construction.

    A. Construction details.
    B. Elevations.
    C. Pictorial presentations.
    D. Furniture plan.

2. _____

3. Which of the following is found on a plot plan?

    A. The direction of joists and major supporting members.
    B. A description of how the structure has been designed to accommodate future expansion.
    C. The location of the house on the site, utilities, and topographical features.
    D. Exterior and interior walls, doors, windows, and built-in cabinets and appliances.

3. _____

4. Which of the following best describes the foundation plan?

    A. Typical orthographic projection showing the exterior features of the building such as the windows and doors, steps, chimney, and other exterior details.
    B. Shows the size and material of the support structure. Gives information pertaining to excavation, waterproofing, and supporting structures.
    C. Locates and identifies plants and other elements on the site surrounding the house.
    D. Shows rafters, ceiling joists, and supporting members.

4. _____

5. This plan shows such features as the hot and cold water system, waste lines, placement of plumbing fixtures, and cleanouts.

    A. Heating and cooling plan.
    B. Plumbing plan.
    C. Electrical plan.
    D. Expansion plan.

5. _____

6. This plan illustrates all exterior and interior walls, doors, windows, patios, walks, decks, fireplaces, and appliances.

    A. Foundation plan.
    B. Furniture plan.
    C. Floor plan.
    D. Roof plan.

6. _____

Part IV: Short Answer/Listing

Provide brief answers to the following questions.

1. The community is a key element in bringing satisfaction and happiness to a homeowner. List eight points to be considered when evaluating a neighborhood. _____

_____

_____

_____

_____

_____

2. List three factors that should be evaluated when examining the price of a building site.

_____

_____

_____

_____

3. What factors should be taken into account if the lot is in a rural location? _____

_____

_____

_____

_____

4. List at least eight individual and family activities that should be provided for in the design of a house. _____

_____

_____

_____

_____

5. The set of construction drawings and the related specifications form the basis for a legal contract between the owner and the builder. Name the types of drawings commonly found in a set of plans. _____

_____

_____

_____

_____

Name _____

Part V: Problems/Activities

1. If you live in a city or town, evaluate your neighborhood on the following points.

   A. Is the neighborhood a well-planned community? _____

   _____

   B. Does the community have room for growth or is it restricted?_____

   _____

   C. Does the community have modern churches, quality schools, and shopping areas? _____

   _____

   D. Is the site near where you work? _____

   E. Is public transportation available and close by? _____

   _____

   F. Is there a high rate of turnover in the neighborhood due to the resale of homes?

   _____

   _____

   G. What are the dimensions of the lot on which your house, condo, or apartment building
      sits? _____

   _____

   H. How many homes are under construction and for sale within a 1/2 mile radius of your
      house, condo, or apartment building? _____

2. Select a floor plan from a magazine, newspaper, or other source and record the square footage
   dedicated to the following activities.

   A. Food preparation _____   I. Sleeping _____

   B. Dining _____   J. Relaxing _____

   C. Entertaining _____   K. Working _____

   D. Recreation _____   L. Storage _____

   E. Hobbies _____   M. Bathing _____

   F. Laundering _____   N. Housekeeping _____

   G. Studying _____   O. Planning _____

   H. Dressing _____   P. Accommodating guests _____

3. Select a site where a new house is being built. (Request permission before entering the site.) Sketch a site plan and show the prominent topographical features such as the contours, elevations, trees, property lines, etc.

Drawing Instruments and Techniques

Text, Pages 67–90

Name _____

Course _____ Date _____ Score _____

Part I: Matching
Match the correct term with its description listed below. Place the corresponding letter on the space provided.

A. Construction lines   E. Freehand sketching
B. Floor plan   F. Grids
C. Plan view   G. Hand pivot method
D. Dimension lines   H. Orthographic projection

1. Lines used to show size and location.   1. _____

2. A method of making a drawing without instruments.   2. _____

3. Drafting aids useful in sketching idea plans, in creating   3. _____
   modular construction drawings, or in drawing
   perspectives.

4. A section view taken about halfway up the wall.   4. _____

5. Very light lines used in the process of creating a   5. _____
   drawing.

6. A means of representing an object from a point at   6. _____
   infinity.

7. A quick and easy method of sketching circles.   7. _____

8. Used as the basis for developing a set of drawings for   8. _____
   a house.

Part II: Multiple Choice
Select the best answer and write the corresponding letter in the space provided.

1. A standard drawing sheet size measuring 9″ × 12″ is   1. _____
   designated by the letter:

   A. A
   B. B
   C. C
   D. D

2. C-size paper is what size?

    A. 12″ × 18″
    B. 18″ × 24″
    C. 24″ × 36″
    D. 36″ × 48″

2. _____

3. In drafting terminology, a "half size" drawing means:

    A. 1/4″ on the drawing equals 1′-0″.
    B. 1/2″ on the drawing equals 1′-0″.
    C. The drawing is only half as large as the object in real life.
    D. None of the above.

3. _____

4. CADD system hard copy output devices include:

    A. Printers.
    B. Pen plotters.
    C. Ink jet plotters.
    D. All of the above.

4. _____

5. Lines used in a floor plan to indicate features above the cutting plane, such as wall cabinets in a kitchen or an archway, are:

    A. Object lines.
    B. Border lines.
    C. Hidden lines.
    D. Centerlines.

5. _____

6. Lines used to indicate the center of holes in symmetrical objects, such as windows and doors, are:

    A. Centerlines.
    B. Hidden lines.
    C. Border lines.
    D. Object lines.

6. _____

Part III: Completion

Complete each sentence with the proper response. Place your answer on the space provided.

1. The three principal views in orthographic projection are the _____, front, and right side views.

1. _____

2. The front view of an object in mechanical drawing is the same as the _____ elevation in architectural drawing.

2. _____

3. The hardness number is printed on the _____ of a wood pencil and along the _____ in mechanical pencils.

3. _____

4. Most architectural drafters use tracing paper, _____, or drafting film.

4. _____

5. T-squares are manufactured from wood, metal, _____, or a combination of these materials.

5. _____

Name _____

6. Drafting tables usually have a _____ machine or straightedge permanently attached for drawing lines.

6. _____

7. Metal protractors with a _____ scale will measure accurately to one minute.

7. _____

8. The divisions of the architect's scale are based on _____ units to the foot, while the divisions of the engineer's scale are based on 10 units to the inch.

8. _____

9. One half scale in architectural drafting means that _____ on the drawing is equal to 1'-0" on the object.

9. _____

10. Use a(n) _____ or H hardness lead in the compass and keep it sharpened to a fine point.

10. _____

11. _____ devices are used when uniformity of letters is essential.

11. _____

12. AEC stands for architectural, _____, and construction.

12. _____

13. Generally, the main storage device on a computer is the _____.

13. _____

14. A _____ plotter produces high-quality drawings using pens or pencils of various colors.

14. _____

15. Thin lines used to show that all of the part is not drawn are _____ break lines.

15. _____

16. _____ lines or crosshatch lines are used to show that the feature has been sectioned.

16. _____

17. Two types of lines that should be drawn lightly and are for the drafter's use only are guidelines and _____ lines. All other lines should be dark in order to reproduce well.

17. _____

Part IV: Short Answer/Listing
Provide brief answers to the following questions.

1. List the elevations that architectural drafters normally draw. _____

_____

_____

2. Why are plastic erasers preferred over pink erasers by many drafters?_____

_____

_____

3. Triangles are used to draw lines that are not horizontal. Name the two triangles most commonly used by drafters. _____

_____

4. Protractors are available in what two styles? _____

_____

5. What are two uses of dividers? _____

_____

_____

6. Briefly explain the procedure for drawing arcs using a compass. _____

_____

_____

_____

7. Briefly explain the procedure for drawing a curve using an irregular curve. _____

_____

_____

_____

8. What two basic types of devices are used to make hard copies of CADD drawings? _____

_____

9. What is the purpose of a drawing? _____

_____

_____

10. Name the type of heavy lines used to show where the object is to be sectioned. _____

_____

11. What is a good rule to follow in spacing words? _____

_____

_____

2.

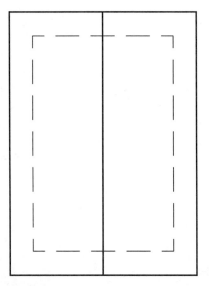

Directions:
Construct the Right Side view of
the object in the space provided.
Be sure to project the heights
from the Front View and transfer
depth dimensions.

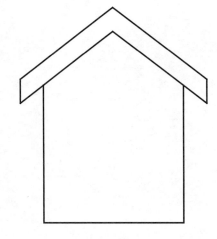

4.

Directions:
Draw each of the lines illustrated below in the space provided to the right of each line. Be sure to pay close attention to the thickness of each line and the size of each element.

Border
line

Object
line

Cutting-
plane line

Short break
line

Hidden
line

Centerline

Long break
line

Leader

5.

Directions:
Practice lettering the alphabet and numbers using a style similar to one illustrated in the text.
Practice "your" style until it becomes comfortable to use.

ARCHITECTURAL LETTERING | NAME: | 4-5

Introduction to Computer-Aided Drafting and Design

5

Text, Pages 91–108

Name _____

Course _____ Date _____ Score _____

Part I: Multiple Choice
Select the best answer and write the corresponding letter in the space provided.

1. A(n) _____ is a collection of standard shapes and symbols typically grouped by application.

    A. material report
    B. hard copy
    C. software command
    D. symbols library

    1. _____

2. Which part of the computer contains the processor, RAM, and input/output interfaces?

    A. Software.
    B. Central processing unit.
    C. Hard copy output device.
    D. Keyboard.

    2. _____

3. The type of software that is usually designed for making typical mechanical drawings is a(n):

    A. General purpose CADD package.
    B. AEC software package.
    C. Windows software.
    D. Special application software.

    3. _____

4. The most common type of input device is:

    A. Roller ball.
    B. Mouse.
    C. Keyboard.
    D. Light pen.

    4. _____

5. _____ is when several stand-alone computer systems are connected to share information.

    A. Scrolling
    B. Networking
    C. Tasking
    D. Tracking

    5. _____

6. The computer hard drive is an example of this device.   6. _____

    A. Tape drive.
    B. Input device.
    C. Floppy disk.
    D. Storage device.

7. Most CADD monitors are: 7. _____

    A. Liquid crystal displays (LCDs).
    B. Pixel mask tubes.
    C. Cathode ray tubes (CRTs).
    D. Flat tension mask tubes.

8. A(n) _____ works with a tablet menu.   8. _____

    A. mouse
    B. light pen
    C. rollerball
    D. joystick

9. A pen plotter plots _____.   9. _____

    A. vectors
    B. raster images
    C. a specialized dot pattern
    D. pixel images

10. When selecting a CADD package, what is the *first* thing you must know?   10. _____

    A. How much it costs.
    B. What you want to accomplish.
    C. Does it have a good reputation.
    D. Is the warranty good.

Part II: Completion
Complete each sentence with the proper response. Place your answer on the space provided.

1. The acronym for computer-aided drafting and design is _____.   1. _____

2. The _____ is the instructions that makes the hardware perform the intended tasks.   2. _____

3. A(n) _____ is a variation of a mouse. It is moved like a mouse, but can have several buttons to activate a variety of functions.   3. _____

4. _____ are like transparent drawing sheets on which you can draw.   4. _____

5. A(n) _____ is related to presentation drawings and shows motion.   5. _____

6. A(n) _____ device is a way to provide the computer with information.   6. _____

Name _____

7. A(n) _____ is a device that transmits data from the CPU to the monitor.

7. _____

8. In CADD, objects are always drawn at their _____ size.

8. _____

9. In order for automatic generation of schedules to work, a drawing must be created with appropriate _____.

9. _____

10. A(n) _____ is a presentation drawing generated by a CADD system that is "shaded" or "colored."

10. _____

Part III: Short Answer/Listing
Provide brief answers to the following questions.

1. List four tasks that a drafter/designer can do using a computer system and the appropriate software. (Example: Plan a part, structure, or other needed product.)

_____

_____

_____

_____

2. What is the overall most important reason to use CADD? _____

3. Which group of commands or functions allow you to change the magnification factor of the view? _____

4. Name four schedules that some CADD packages can produce automatically to be part of a set of construction drawings.

_____

_____

5. Name four objects (basic elements) that are used to create drawings. _____

_____

_____

6. List four units of measure that most CADD programs support. _____

_____

_____

7. List four common title symbols that are generally included in an AEC CADD package.

_____

_____

8. Name three methods of generating walls that are used by typical AEC CADD programs.

_____

_____

Part IV: Problems/Activities

1.

Directions:
Connect each of the general purpose CADD characteristics on the left with the appropriate example on the right.

Basic System ☐	☐ CPU, Input/Output Devices
Computer Components ☐	☐ Copy, Erase, Move, Scale
Storage Devices ☐	☐ Transparent Drawing Sheets
Objects ☐	☐ Decimal Degrees, Radians
Object Editing ☐	☐ Hard Drive, Floppy
Layers ☐	☐ Surface, Solid
Standard Linetypes ☐	☐ CADD Workstation
Angular Units ☐	☐ Area, Distance, Angle
Display Controls ☐	☐ Continuous, Dashed, Hidden
Drawing Aids ☐	☐ Lines, Points, Circles
Geometric Analysis ☐	☐ Zoom, Pan, View
3D Models ☐	☐ Grid, Snap, Ortho

GENERAL PURPOSE CADD	NAME:	5-1

2.

Directions:
Draw a line from each of the AEC CADD characteristics on the left to the matching example on the right.

Rendering ☐   ☐ Surface and Solid Models

Space Diagram ☐   ☐ Mapping, Site Development

3D Capability ☐   ☐ Tub, Lavatory, Shower

Plumbing Symbols ☐   ☐ Concrete in Section

Electrical Symbols ☐   ☐ Presentation Drawing

HVAC Symbols ☐   ☐ Display Grid

Tree and Plant Symbols ☐   ☐ Switches, Outlets, Meter

Title Symbols ☐   ☐ Automatic Wall Thickness

Hatch Patterns ☐   ☐ Heating, Ventilating & AC

Drawing Aids ☐   ☐ Personalized Lettering Style

Schedule Generation ☐   ☐ North Arrow, Scale, Tags

Custom Font ☐   ☐ DXF Format, Lotus 1-2-3

Data Exchange ☐   ☐ Window, Door, Lighting

AEC CADD CHARACTERISTICS	NAME:	5-2

6 CADD Commands and Functions

Text, Pages 109–127

Name _____

Course _____ Date _____ Score _____

Part I: Short Answer/Listing
Provide brief answers to the following questions.

1. What purpose do drawing commands serve? _____

2. In what ways may commands be entered? _____

3. List five drawing commands. _____

4. When are editing commands used? _____

5. Which editing command should be used to permanently remove objects from the drawing?

6. Explain how the **COPY** command differs from the **MOVE** command. _____

7. When is the **DOUBLE LINE** command useful? _____

8. Name the three functions that the display control commands provide. _____

Copyright by Goodheart-Willcox Co., Inc.

9. Identify the display control commands typically found in CADD packages. _____

_____

_____

10. List the five basic types of dimensioning commands. _____

_____

_____

_____

11. Which three common commands are used to change an object's display color? _____

_____

12. What purpose does a display grid serve? _____

_____

13. List the five general groups of CADD commands. _____

_____

_____

_____

_____

_____

14. In general, what do inquiry commands allow you to do? _____

_____

_____

Part II: Multiple Choice

Select the best answer and write the corresponding letter in the space provided.

1. Which of the following commands may be used to change the orientation or size of an object?

   1. _____

   A. **COPY.**
   B. **AREA.**
   C. **MOVE.**
   D. None of the above.

2. Specifying a starting point, center, and end point is one method of drawing a(n):

   2. _____

   A. Line.
   B. Circle.
   C. Arc.
   D. Rectangle.

Name _____

3. To draw a rectangle, generally you can pick opposite corners or specify the _____.

    A. location
    B. width and height
    C. thickness
    D. rotation

3. _____

4. With _____, you pick a starting point and specify a displacement from that point.

    A. relative displacement
    B. offset displacement
    C. projected displacement
    D. extended displacement

4. _____

5. The **ROTATE** command may be used to:

    A. Move entities to a new location on the drawing.
    B. Alter the orientation of entities on a drawing.
    C. Draw a mirror image of an object.
    D. All of the above.

5. _____

6. The command that trims two lines and then connects the trimmed ends with a new straight line is the _____ command.

    A. **FILLET**
    B. **CHAMFER**
    C. **ROTATE**
    D. **SCALE**

6. _____

7. The **LIST** command enables the drafter to:

    A. Show the data related to an object.
    B. Measure the distance and angle between two points.
    C. Generate copies of a specific object.
    D. None of the above.

7. _____

8. The _____ command is used to increase or decrease the magnification factor.

    A. **VIEW**
    B. **PAN**
    C. **ZOOM**
    D. **REDRAW**

8. _____

9. The process of measuring and identifying lengths, distances, or angles between objects is:

    A. Finding area.
    B. Editing.
    C. Dimensioning.
    D. All of the above.

9. _____

10. The function of the **LEADER** command is to:

    A. Regenerate a program.
    B. Connect dimensions to objects.
    C. Add a specific or local note.
    D. All of the above.

10. _____

11. Which of the following statements applies to layers?

    A. Layers are similar to opaque overlays.
    B. Most software packages provide six layers.
    C. Each layer has a different zoom factor.
    D. Objects can be drawn on different layers.

11. _____

12. A drawing aid helpful for connecting objects very accurately is:

    A. **GRID**
    B. **AXIS**
    C. **SNAP**
    D. None of the above.

12. _____

13. A 3D model that has volume is a:

    A. Solid model.
    B. Surface model.
    C. Shaded model.
    D. All of the above.

13. _____

14. To protect a drawing in the event of a power loss, use the _____ command often.

    A. **WINDOW**
    B. **STATUS**
    C. **DRAW**
    D. **SAVE**

14. _____

Part III: Completion

Complete each sentence with the proper response. Place your answer on the space provided.

1. The _____ of a line include linetype, width, or color.

1. _____

2. Specifying a _____ and diameter is one method used to draw a circle.

2. _____

3. Calculating distances, areas, and perimeters is a function of an _____ command.

3. _____

4. A line may be lengthened to meet a boundary edge using the _____ command.

4. _____

5. The _____ command makes a number of copies of an object in a circular or rectangular pattern.

5. _____

6. When it is necessary to repeatedly move back and forth between views on a drawing, the _____ command should be used.

6. _____

Name _____

7. Marker blips are removed by the _____ command.

7. _____

8. **LINEAR**, **ANGULAR**, **DIAMETER**, **RADIUS**, and **LEADER** are basic types of _____ commands.

8. _____

9. _____, including **GRID**, **SNAP**, and **ORTHO**, increase drawing accuracy and save time.

9. _____

10. Hidden lines in 3D view may be removed using the _____ command.

10. _____

11. Which command may be used to reverse the action of the previous command?

11. _____

Part IV: Matching

Match the correct term with its description listed below. Place the corresponding letter on the space provided.

A. **ANGULAR**
B. **ARC**
C. Blocks
D. **DIAMETER**
E. **FILLET**
F. **HATCH**
G. **LINE**
H. Object snap
I. **PAN**
J. Regular polygon
K. **SCALE**
L. Surface modeling

1. The most basic drawing command.

1. _____

2. A command that draws partial circles.

2. _____

3. An object with equal sides and included angles.

3. _____

4. A command that creates patterns for hatching.

4. _____

5. The size of an existing object may be increased or decreased with this command.

5. _____

6. A command that produces a smoothly fitted arc of a certain radius between two lines, arcs, or circles.

6. _____

7. Moves the drawing in the display window from one location to another.

7. _____

8. A type of dimension that shows the angle between two nonparallel lines.

8. _____

9. Used to dimension circles.

9. _____

10. A 3D representation of an object that is a "skin" over a wireframe.

10. _____

11. Special objects that can be inserted into a drawing.

11. _____

12. Locks the cursor onto locations on existing objects.

12. _____

Part V: Problems/Activities

1. **Display Control Commands and Drawing Aids.** This assignment requires the use of a CADD system. Practice using the display control commands and drawing aids to develop your ability to use the CADD system. Study the documentation for each command before using it. Practice using the commands until you thoroughly understand their application.

2.

Directions:
This assignment requires the use of a CADD system. Using a scale of 1/4″ = 1′-0″ and an A-, B-, or C-size drawing sheet, draw a border line 480″@90°, 348″@0°, 480″@270°, and 348″@180°. The title block is 12″ high and the plate number box is 36″ wide. This matches the border shown here. Then, use the following drawing commands (or your software's equivalent) to draw the lines and shapes indicated.

Line

Arc

Circle

Polygon

Rectangle

Double line

Hatch

Text

Add the title, assignment number, and your name to the title block.

DRAWING COMMANDS	NAME:	6-2

3.

Directions:
This assignment requires the use of a CADD system. Using a scale of 1/4" = 1'-0", prepare a drawing sheet identical to the one required for Problem/Assignment 6-2. This assignment deals with selected editing and inquiry commands. Practice using all of the commands that your CADD software provides, but demonstrate the use of the following.

Draw a circle at one location and move it to another.

Draw a rectangle and make two copies of it.

Draw one-half of a geometric shape and mirror the other side to complete the shape.

Draw a shape and rotate it 15°.

Draw a box and use the FILLET command to round the corners.

Draw a three-sided figure as shown and extend it to twice its original length.

Use the ARRAY command to create five circles around a center point.

Use the SCALE command to change the size of a circle to half of its original size.

Draw a rectangle and use the AREA command to determine its area.

EDITING AND INQUIRY COMMANDS	NAME:	6-3

4.

Directions:

This assignment requires the use of a CADD system. Using a scale of 1/4″ = 1′-0″, prepare a drawing sheet identical to the one required for Problem/Assignment 6-2. Draw a series of rectangles within the border leaving room for dimensions. Using the appropriate dimensioning commands, dimension the length and width of each rectangle. You may wish to add other shapes to show angular, diameter, radius, and leader dimensions as well.

| DIMENSIONING COMMANDS | NAME: | 6-4 |

Room Planning—Sleeping Area and Bath Facilities

7

Text, Pages 129–147

Name _____

Course _____ Date _____ Score _____

Part I: Multiple Choice
Select the best answer and write the corresponding letter in the space provided.

1. Approximately _____ of the house is devoted to the sleeping area, which includes bedrooms, baths, dressing rooms, and nurseries.

   A. 1/2
   B. 1/4
   C. 1/3
   D. 3/4

   1. _____

2. The _____ normally determines the number of bedrooms a house will have.

   A. size of the family
   B. size of the neighborhood
   C. number of guests
   D. None of the above.

   2. _____

3. Generally, _____ homes have the most sales potential.

   A. one-bedroom
   B. two-bedroom
   C. three-bedroom
   D. four-bedroom

   3. _____

4. In a split bedroom plan, the _____ is separated from the remaining bedrooms for additional privacy.

   A. smallest bedroom
   B. nursery
   C. guest bedroom
   D. master bedroom

   4. _____

5. The Federal Housing Administration recommends that the minimum size for a bedroom should be _____ square feet.

   A. 50
   B. 100
   C. 150
   D. 200

   5. _____

6. When designing bedroom space for the disabled, a
   clear space of _____ square is usually required for
   turning a wheelchair in front of a closet.

   A. 3'
   B. 5'
   C. 7'
   D. 9'

6. _____

7. The minimum bedroom closet depth is _____.

   A. 16"
   B. 20"
   C. 24"
   D. 28"

7. _____

8. The most desirable location for a closet is _____.

   A. on an outside wall
   B. in the hall near the bedroom
   C. near the bedroom entrance
   D. None of the above.

8. _____

9. Bifold, _____, or sliding closet doors generally allow
   for partial entry by wheelchair users.

   A. split
   B. ribbon
   C. 1/2
   D. accordion

9. _____

10. An ideal bedroom will have windows _____.

    A. on two walls
    B. on one wall
    C. low on the wall
    D. evenly spaced on the walls

10. _____

11. Bedroom doors should be _____ wide to accommodate
    a wheelchair.

    A. 2'-6"
    B. 2'-8"
    C. 2'-10"
    D. 3'-0"

11. _____

12. The best location for a bedroom door is _____.

    A. on a long wall
    B. near a corner
    C. in the center of a wall
    D. on an exterior wall

12. _____

Name _____

Part II: Completion
Complete each sentence with the proper response. Place your answer on the space provided.

1. Two-story and split-level house designs require at least _____ baths.

1. _____

2. A water closet and lavatory comprise a _____ bath.

2. _____

3. A water closet, lavatory, and shower generally comprise a _____ bath.

3. _____

4. A minimum size bath is _____ by 8'.

4. _____

5. If a bidet is included in the design of a home, it is often installed in the _____ bath.

5. _____

6. A well-lighted _____ should be placed above the bathroom lavatory.

6. _____

7. Provide space at least _____ wide for a water closet.

7. _____

8. The most popular size for a bathtub is _____.

8. _____

9. Prefabricated shower stalls are available in metal, _____, and plastic.

9. _____

10. More luxurious showers are usually made of _____, terrazzo, or marble.

10. _____

11. Bathroom storage and countertop space can be provided by installing sink cabinets or _____.

11. _____

12. In larger baths, some _____ may be used as a whirlpool or a bathtub.

12. _____

13. If an exhaust fan is used in a bath, it should be located near the tub and _____ area.

13. _____

14. Electrical switches in a bath should be placed out of reach from the _____.

14. _____

15. _____ receptacles installed in bathrooms are fast-acting devices that detect short circuits and immediately shut off power to the receptacle.

15. _____

16. Bathroom doors are generally 2'-6" or 2'-4" in width, but need to be at least _____ wide for wheelchair access.

16. _____

Part III: Short Answer/Listing

Provide brief answers to the following questions.

1. List the steps in planning the furniture arrangement of a bedroom using a CADD system.

   _____

   _____

   _____

   _____

2. Name three reasons why the decor of a bathroom should be well-planned. _____

   _____

   _____

   _____

3. Name three planning considerations to make in order to provide safety in the bath. _____

   _____

   _____

   _____

   _____

4. In addition to the normal activities carried out in the bathroom, list two others a larger bath might accommodate. _____

   _____

5. Name three basic areas of a home. _____

   _____

   _____

6. What is the recommended distance from the rim of the bathroom sink to the floor for wheelchair armrests? _____

7. What is the recommended height of a water closet seat for wheelchair users? _____

   _____

Room Planning—Living Area

Text, Pages 149–187

Name _____

Course _____ Date _____ Score _____

Part I: Completion
Complete each sentence with the proper response. Place your answer on the space provided.

1. An average-size living room contains approximately _____ square feet.

   1. _____

2. Analyzing the functions to be performed in the living room helps determine the _____ needed.

   2. _____

3. To discourage "through traffic," slightly raise or lower the living room _____.

   3. _____

4. Locating the living room at grade level lets activities flow to outside _____ or terraces.

   4. _____

5. Rather than opening up directly to an outside entry, the living room should open up to a _____ or hallway.

   5. _____

6. Locate a living room on the _____ side of the house in warm climates to take advantage of shaded, cooler areas.

   6. _____

7. Using large windows or _____ doors increases a feeling of "spaciousness."

   7. _____

8. The living room should be located near the _____ room and the family room.

   8. _____

9. An informal _____ such as a flower planter, furniture arrangement, screen, or change in level may serve to separate the dining and living rooms.

   9. _____

10. To minimize the weak points and emphasize the good points of a room, use color, _____, and design.

    10. _____

Part II: Multiple Choice
Select the best answer and write the corresponding letter in the space provided.

1. A small dining room would require approximately _____ square feet to seat four people.

   1. _____

   A. 100
   B. 120
   C. 140
   D. 160

2. A medium-size dining room should seat _____ people.

    A. 6 to 8
    B. 8 to 10
    C. 10 to 12
    D. 12 to 14

2. _____

3. Allow _____ between the back of the chairs and the wall for serving in the dining room.

    A. 1'-0"
    B. 2'-0"
    C. 3'-0"
    D. 4'-0"

3. _____

4. An ideal dining room location would be one between the _____ and the kitchen.

    A. foyer
    B. master bedroom
    C. living room
    D. utility room

4. _____

5. A(n) _____ makes the rooms appear larger.

    A. two-story plan
    B. ranch-style plan
    C. closed plan
    D. open plan

5. _____

6. The color scheme in the dining room is frequently the same as that in the _____.

    A. living room
    B. kitchen
    C. bedroom
    D. bathroom

6. _____

7. To enable persons in wheelchairs to use the dining room, a minimum of _____ is needed for passing between furniture pieces and/or walls.

    A. 24"
    B. 28"
    C. 32"
    D. 36"

7. _____

8. A _____ entry should be impressive because it is the first part of the house that guests see. It should be centrally located to provide easy access to various parts of the house.

    A. special-purpose
    B. main
    C. service
    D. side

8. _____

Name _____

9. The entry door in a wheelchair-accessible home should have a clearing space of _____ around it.

   A. 22″
   B. 26″
   C. 30″
   D. 34″

9. _____

Part III: Matching
Match the correct term with its description listed below. Place the corresponding letter on the space provided.

A. Court
B. Deck
C. Double doors
D. Entry
E. Recreation room
F. Foyer

G. Mudroom
H. Patio
I. Play patio
J. Porch
K. Sliding doors

1. Its style should be compatible with the remainder of the house.

1. _____

2. Used to place more emphasis on the entry and increase its function.

2. _____

3. Can be added between the service entry and the kitchen to improve the overall design.

3. _____

4. Generally used in special-purpose entries.

4. _____

5. Where guests are greeted and coats are removed.

5. _____

6. Its purpose is to provide a place where the family can play or pursue hobbies.

6. _____

7. Located at ground level near the house, but not structurally connected to it.

7. _____

8. Generally designed for use by children and adults for physical activities that require more open space.

8. _____

9. Raised above grade level and structurally connected to the house.

9. _____

10. An uncovered porch.

10. _____

11. Area totally or partially enclosed by walls or a roof.

11. _____

Part IV: Short Answer/Listing

Provide brief answers to the following questions.

1. Name five rooms that are generally considered to be part of the living area. _____
   _____
   _____
   _____

2. List five questions you should address when planning a living room. _____
   _____
   _____
   _____
   _____
   _____

3. What three factors affect the dining room size? _____
   _____
   _____
   _____

4. What pieces of furniture are frequently used in the dining room? _____
   _____
   _____
   _____

5. Name two ways in which protection from the weather can be provided for in an entry.
   _____
   _____

6. List four factors that should determine the size of the foyer. _____
   _____
   _____
   _____

7. Name four places where a family recreation room is generally located. _____
   _____
   _____
   _____

8. When should rugs and deep pile carpeting *not* be used in a family recreation room?
   _____
   _____

Name _____

9. Name four types of special-purpose rooms. _____

_____

_____

_____

10. What requirements should be considered when planning a special-purpose room such as a darkroom? _____

_____

_____

_____

11. List three types of activities normally performed on patios. _____

_____

_____

12. List four popular materials used in constructing patios. _____

_____

_____

13. Where should relaxing patios be located? _____

_____

14. Will a living or entertaining patio most likely be located to the front or back of the house?

_____

15. What features are sometimes added to porches in northern climates to increase their usefulness? _____

3.

Directions:
Complete the entry/foyer below by adding a slate floor, a brick veneer exterior, an entry arrow, a plant in the foyer, and a closet shelf and rod.

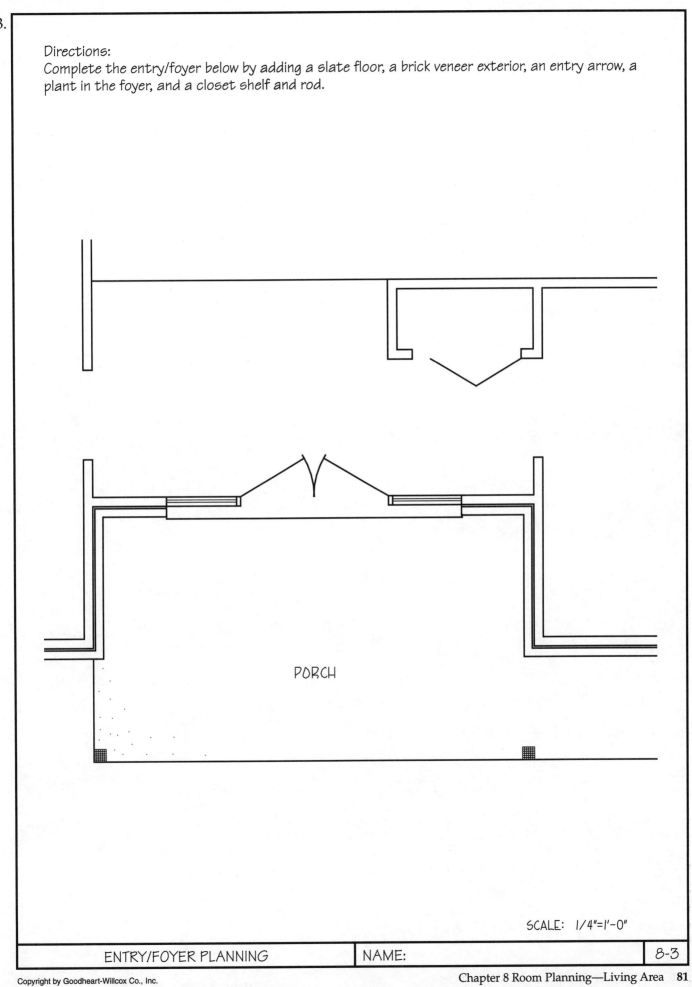

PORCH

SCALE: 1/4"=1'-0"

ENTRY/FOYER PLANNING	NAME:	8-3

4.

Directions:
Plan a functional arrangement of furniture in the family recreation room below. Include a sofa, upholstered chair, coffee table, lamp table and lamp, and built-in cabinets along the wall opposite the fireplace. Draw an elevation view of the storage units in the space provided.

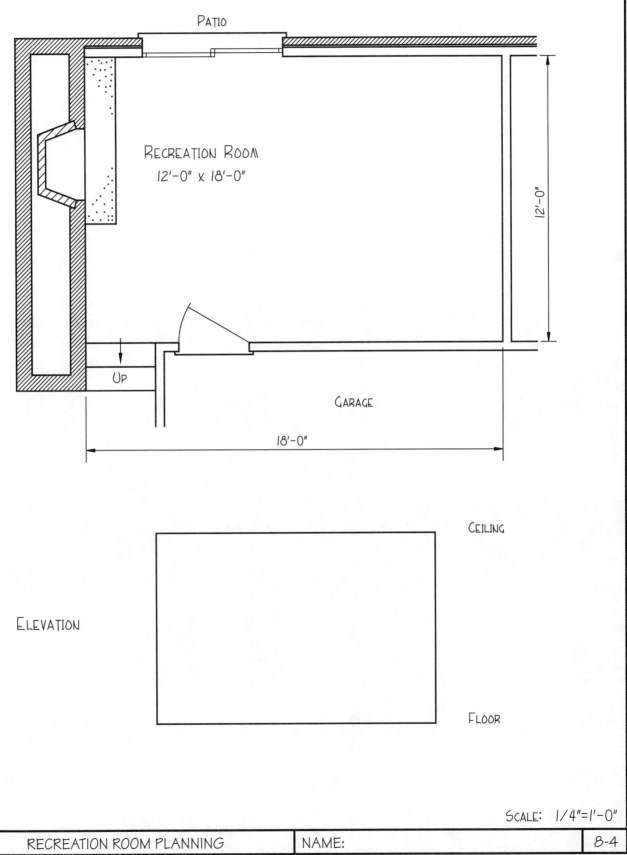

PATIO

RECREATION ROOM
12'-0" x 18'-0"

12'-0"

UP

GARAGE

18'-0"

CEILING

ELEVATION

FLOOR

SCALE: 1/4"=1'-0"

| RECREATION ROOM PLANNING | NAME: | 8-4 |

5.

Directions:
Using the plan below, complete the covered porch on the right and patio on the left. Include clay tile pavers on the porch, a concrete patio divided into a 4'-0" square grid, seating along the long porch wall, two lounge chairs and a round table on the patio, plants along the front privacy wall, a hedge between the living room and patio, and several plants in pots on the patio and porch.

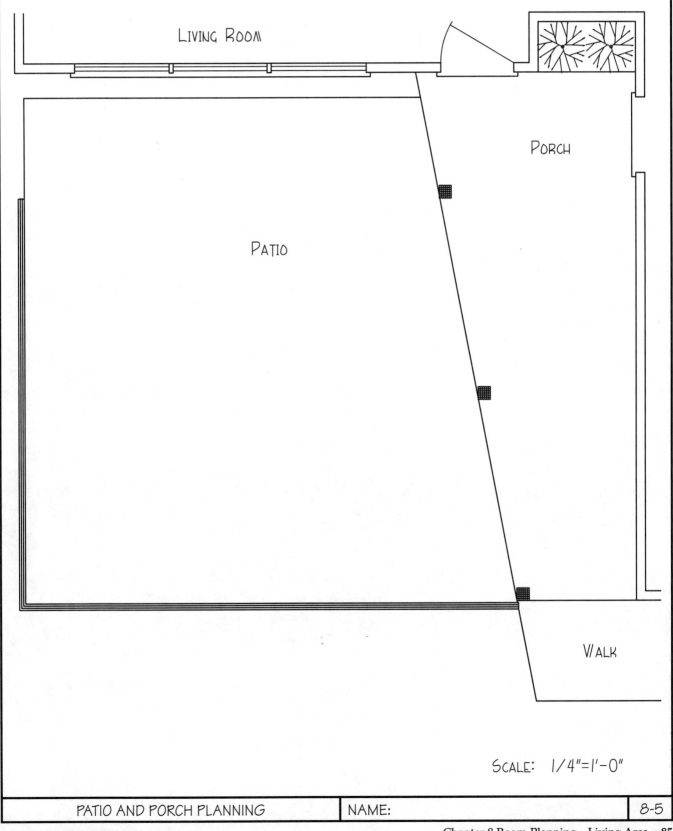

LIVING ROOM

PORCH

PATIO

WALK

SCALE: 1/4"=1'-0"

| PATIO AND PORCH PLANNING | NAME: | 8-5 |

Room Planning—Service Area

9

Text, Pages 189–214

Name _____

Course _____ Date _____ Score _____

Part I: Matching
Match the correct term with its description listed below. Place the corresponding letter on the space provided.

  A. Corridor kitchen
  B. Island kitchen
  C. L-shaped kitchen

  D. Peninsula kitchen
  E. Straight-line kitchen
  F. U-shaped kitchen

1. A popular kitchen design for cottages and apartments.

1. _____

2. A compact work triangle, reduced traffic, and ease of joining to a dining room are features of this kitchen design.

2. _____

3. A variation of the straight-line, L-shaped, or U-shaped kitchen.

3. _____

4. A kitchen design that maintains a high level of efficiency. The most popular of the six kitchen designs.

4. _____

5. A kitchen design located along two adjacent walls.

5. _____

6. A kitchen design located on two walls opposite each other.

6. _____

Part II: Multiple Choice
Select the best answer and write the corresponding letter in the space provided.

1. The standard kitchen base cabinet is _____.

1. _____

  A. 36" high and 24" deep with a width in 2" increments
  B. 30" high and 25" deep with a width in 4" increments
  C. 36" high and 23" deep with a width in 3" increments
  D. 34-1/2" high and 24" deep with a width in 3" increments

2. When designing a kitchen to be handicapped accessible, toe space of _____ deep and 8" to 11" high is needed under the cabinets for wheelchair footrests.

   A. 3"
   B. 6"
   C. 9"
   D. 12"

2. _____

3. The space designed for a two-car garage should range in size from _____.

   A. 11′ × 19′ to 16′ × 25′
   B. 20′ × 20′ to 25′ × 25′
   C. 12′ × 18′ to 14′ × 24′
   D. 15′ × 20′ to 22′ × 22′

3. _____

4. To be handicapped accessible, a width of _____ is recommended for one car and a wheelchair in a garage.

   A. 8′ to 10-1/2′
   B. 10′ to 12-1/2′
   C. 12′ to 14-1/2′
   D. 14′ to 16-1/2′

4. _____

5. A two-car garage door is generally _____.

   A. 16′ wide and 7′ high
   B. 12′ wide and 7′ high
   C. 8′ wide and 7′ high
   D. 14′ wide and 8′ high

5. _____

Part III: Completion
Complete each sentence with the proper response. Place your answer on the space provided.

1. The kitchen is usually the _____ expensive area of the home per square foot.

1. _____

2. The kitchen work triangle should not exceed _____ feet.

2. _____

3. Pots and pans should be stored near the _____ center rather than the food preparation center.

3. _____

4. To adapt a kitchen design for a person in a wheelchair, the work surfaces should be _____, sinks should have clearance underneath, and cooking units should be accessible.

4. _____

5. Most of the kitchen storage space is available in kitchen _____.

5. _____

6. On a drawing, wall cabinets are shown with _____, while base cabinets are shown as object lines.

6. _____

7. A kitchen eating area should be located outside the _____ area, but convenient to it.

7. _____

Name _____

8. If chairs are to be used at a kitchen eating counter, the height of the counter should be _____ inches.

8. _____

9. _____ may be satisfactory in warmer climates, while garages are more commonly built in colder climates.

9. _____

10. A covered walkway should be provided from a free-standing garage to the _____ entrance.

10. _____

11. Recreational vehicles may require garage doors higher than _____ feet.

11. _____

12. The minimum driveway width for a single-car garage is _____ feet.

12. _____

13. To avoid backing directly onto the street from a garage or carport, a _____ should be provided.

13. _____

Part IV: Short Answer/Listing
Provide brief answers to the following questions.

1. List the five rooms or areas included in the service area. _____

_____

_____

_____

2. List the three work centers found in the kitchen. _____

_____

_____

3. The work triangle is one measure of kitchen efficiency. Explain the procedure for measuring the work triangle. _____

_____

_____

_____

4. Where should lighting be provided in the kitchen? _____

_____

_____

_____

5. What is the purpose of a clothes care center? _____

_____

_____

_____

6. Name three factors that determine the size and location of a garage or carport. _____

_____

_____

7. List four factors to consider when designing or constructing garages. _____

_____

_____

_____

2.

Directions:
Study the configuration of this large, complex kitchen to determine the most functional layout. Include a refrigerator, range, dishwasher, planning desk, sink, and breakfast bar with cabinets above and stools below. Show a ceramic tile floor as a 12" square grid. Label appliances.

9-2

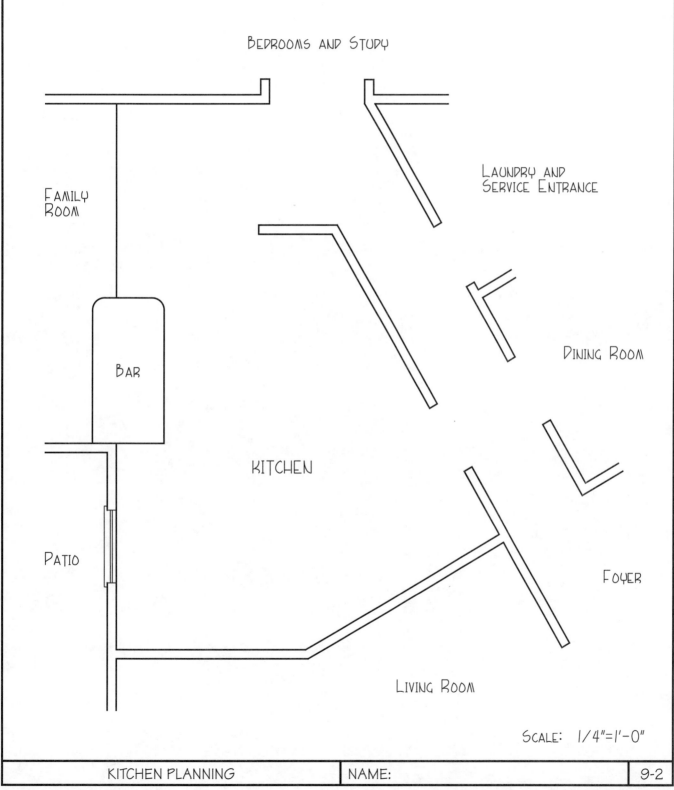

BEDROOMS AND STUDY

LAUNDRY AND
SERVICE ENTRANCE

FAMILY
ROOM

BAR

DINING ROOM

KITCHEN

PATIO

FOYER

LIVING ROOM

SCALE: 1/4"=1'-0"

| KITCHEN PLANNING | NAME: | 9-2 |

3. **Kitchen Design.** This assignment will be evaluated based on the following factors: Quality of work; the degree to which the design meets parameters; quality of communication through proper use of symbols, notes, and standard layout; and neatness of the print.

Directions: You are to design a modern U-shaped kitchen that applies the principles of good design as described in the text. Present a floor plan, an elevation of each wall, a typical section through the cabinets along one wall from floor to ceiling, and a cabinet and appliance schedule. Draw the plan view and elevations at 1/2″ = 1′-0″ scale and the typical section at 1″ = 1′-0″ scale. Make your drawings on two C-size sheets divided into four 9″ × 12″ areas. Place one drawing in each of the 9″ × 12″ areas. Make a print of the completed drawings and cut into 9″ × 12″ sheets. Bind the pages along one edge. Use a title page as the cover.

Specifications. Include the following elements in your design:

- Utilize a floor area of between 125 and 200 square feet.

- Appliances should include a cooking top and oven (separate or combined), and a refrigerator, sink, garbage disposal, and dishwasher.

- Use standard manufactured base and wall cabinets.

- Include a range hood over the cooking area and incorporate at least one window in the kitchen. Show the work triangle (not to exceed 22′) and identify the total length.

- Dimension the finished wall to finished wall sizes on the plan view.

- Incorporate a soffit area above the wall cabinets for down lighting or a dropped ceiling. Show all appropriate dimensions on the typical wall section. Refer to Figure 9-20 in the text.

- Obtain manufacturer's spec sheets for the specifications of cabinets and appliances. You must use real dimensions for this assignment. Prepare an appliance and cabinet schedule that includes the following: Number of each item, manufacturer's identification, make or model, and price, if available.

5.

Directions:
The pictorial shows a detached garage of frame construction. Draw a plan view of this garage assuming the following: The garage is 22'-0" long by 20'-0" wide, the door is 16'-0" wide, a 3'-0" side door leads to the house, the garage has two windows on the left side, and shelves are located at the rear of the garage. The garage walls are 5 1/4" thick. Draw the garage at 1/4"=1'-0" scale.

6.

Directions:
Plan a driveway with a turnaround that meets the following criteria. The drive is 18'-0" wide at the garage with a turning radius beginning 6'-0" in front of the garage on the right side. The turnaround is 20'-0" wide and proceeds 6'-0" beyond the turning radius tangent point. The width of the drive between the turnaround and street is 10'-0". Show all tangent points, centers, and dimensions.

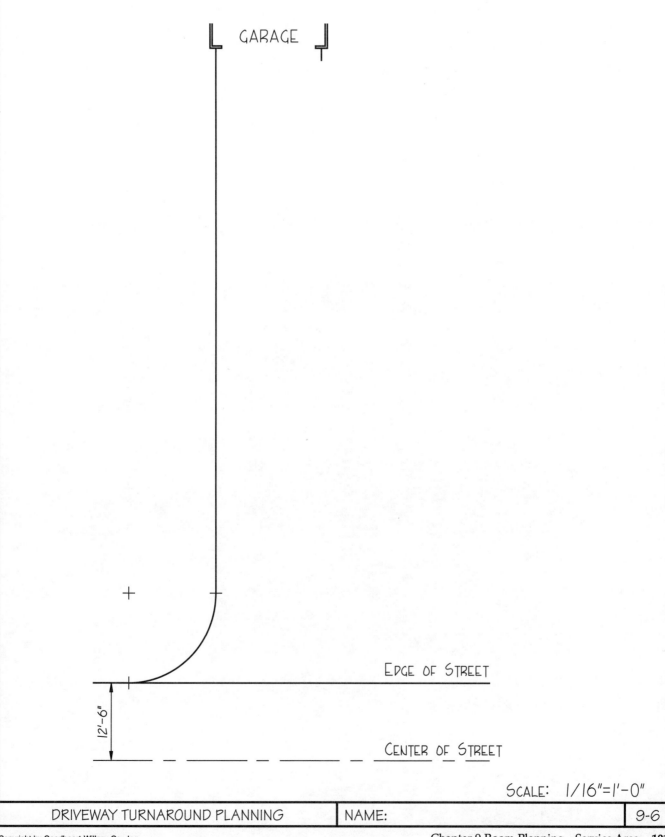

GARAGE

EDGE OF STREET

12'-6"

CENTER OF STREET

SCALE: 1/16"=1'-0"

| DRIVEWAY TURNAROUND PLANNING | NAME: | 9-6 |

Plot Plans
10

Text, Pages 217–232

Name _____

Course _____ Date _____ Score _____

Part I: Matching
Match the correct term with its description listed below. Place the corresponding letter on the space provided.

A. Bearing angles
B. Benchmark
C. Blue
D. Closed contour lines
E. Contour interval
F. Contour line
G. Estimated contours

H. Green
I. Landscape plan
J. Meridian arrow
K. Plot plan
L. Property lines
M. Topographical features

1. Plan view drawing that shows the site and location of buildings on the property.

1. _____

2. Lines that define the site boundaries.

2. _____

3. Recorded in degrees—sometimes including minutes and seconds—from either north or south.

3. _____

4. Identified with a special symbol on a plot plan when a property corner begins or ends here.

4. _____

5. A line connecting points that have the same elevation.

5. _____

6. The vertical distance between two adjacent contours.

6. _____

7. Represent summits and depressions.

7. _____

8. Represented by a short dashed line similar to a hidden line.

8. _____

9. Include trees, ground cover, railroad tracks, sewer lines, fences, water, and sand.

9. _____

10. Color that represents water (streams, lakes, marshes, ponds) on topographical drawings.

10. _____

11. Color that represents vegetation on topographical drawings.

11. _____

12. Known as the north symbol.

12. _____

13. Illustrates the type and placement of trees, shrubs, flowers, gardens, and pools on the site.

13. _____

Part II: Short Answer/Listing
Provide brief answers to the following questions.

1. List the features found on a plot plan. _____
_____
_____
_____
_____
_____
_____
_____
_____

2. Describe the procedure for drawing the property lines of a given site. _____
_____
_____
_____

3. Which type of line is used to represent contours drawn as a result of a survey? _____
_____

4. Which features on a topographical drawing are represented in black? _____
_____

5. What does brown represent on topographical drawings? _____
_____

6. During the analysis of a site, which items must be considered to determine the location and placement of the structure? _____
_____
_____
_____
_____
_____
_____
_____

7. Name three methods of representing the house on the plot plan. _____
_____
_____
_____

8. When following the procedure for drawing a plot plan, which step comes after you have lightly drawn the contour lines? _____
_____
_____

9. At what point should contour lines be darkened on a plot plan? _____

_____

_____

10. What information is given on a landscape plan that is also given on a plot plan? _____

_____

_____

_____

_____

_____

Part III: Completion
Complete each sentence with the proper response. Place your answer on the space provided.

1. The plot plan is drawn from information supplied by a(n) _____ and recorded on a site plan.

1. _____

2. Property line lengths are measured with a(n) _____ scale to the nearest 1/100 foot.

2. _____

3. _____ lines help describe the topography of a site by depicting the shape and elevation of the land.

3. _____

4. _____ elevations are usually acceptable in residential home construction.

4. _____

5. A(n) _____ slope is indicated when contours are placed close together.

5. _____

6. When contours are smooth and parallel, the ground surface is _____.

6. _____

7. _____ contours indicate rough and uneven ground surface.

7. _____

8. Contours of _____ elevations do not touch.

8. _____

9. Contours cross watersheds and ridges at _____ angles.

9. _____

10. When the distance between the house and property line is critical, the _____ of the roof should be shown on the drawing.

10. _____

11. To dimension the location of the house on the site, dimension the distance from the _____ of the exterior wall to the property line.

11. _____

12. Scales commonly used in drawing plot plans range from 1/8″ = 1′-0″ to _____.

12. _____

Part IV: Problems/Activities

1.

Directions:
Draw the proper topographical symbol in the space provided.

Sand	Gravel	Dry clay

Open woodland	Dense forest	Orchard

Tall grass	Marsh	Large stones

Oak tree   Pine tree   Spot elevation

Fence   Property line

Paved road   Telephone line

Water line   Contour line

Septic field   Power line

TOPOGRAPHICAL SYMBOLS   NAME: 10-1

2.

Directions:
Plot the following property line directions (bearings) in the circle as shown. Note the direction of north is generally toward the top of the drawing, but this may be any direction desired. Label each line showing its bearing.

N 15° E	S 32° 30′ W
N 90° 0′ 0″ E	S 78° 15′ W
S 75° E	N 90° W
Due South	N 45° W

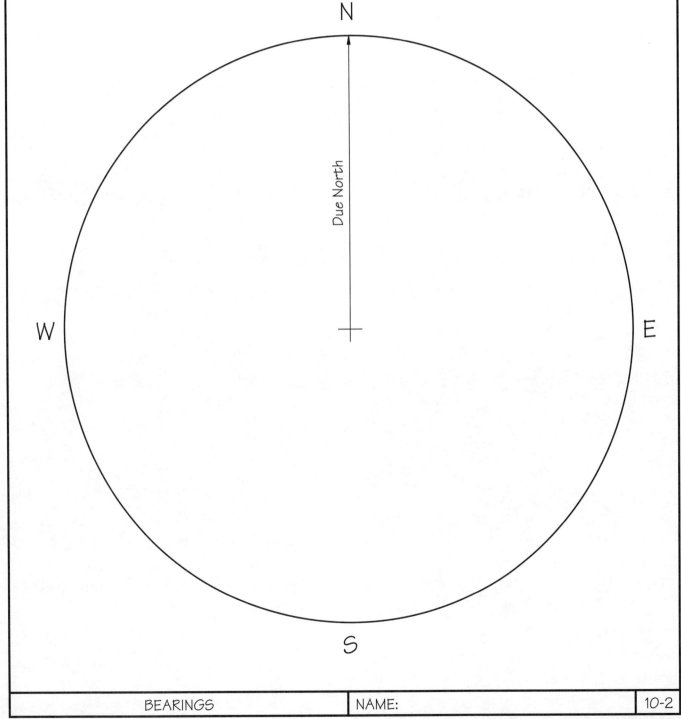

N

Due North

W

E

S

3.

Directions:

Using the property line symbol and format shown in the example below, locate the property boundaries described in the chart. Note the scale and direction of north.

> Begin at point A.
> Line AB bears Due North for a distance of 150.0'.
> Line BC bears N 75° E for a distance of 112.5'.
> Line CD bears S 56° E for a distance of 45.0'.
> Line DE bears S 15° W for a distance of 142.5'.
> Determine the bearing and length of line EA.
> Label property lines and corners.

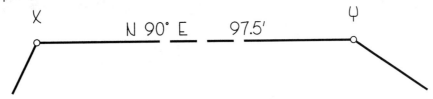

X   N 90° E   97.5'   Y

A×

4.

Directions:
This assignment consists of two parts—plotting contour lines from an elevation grid and showing a profile section defined by a cutting plane. Using the elevation grid at the top of the page, plot the contour lines at elevations 5, 10, and 15 feet. Use the proper contour line symbol and label. Draw a profile section of the property defined by Section A1,1 in the space provided. Be sure to project the points from the grid above. Hatch the sectioned area in the profile.

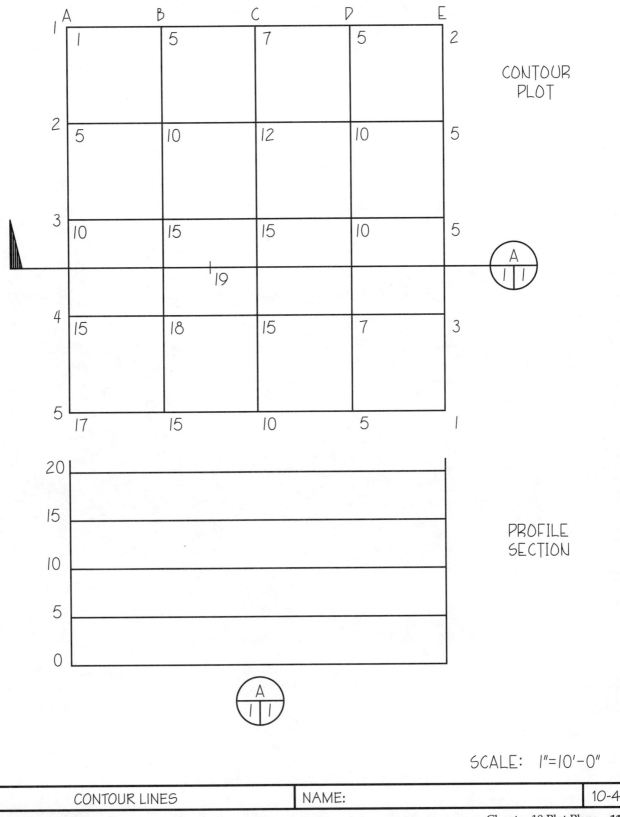

CONTOUR PLOT

PROFILE SECTION

SCALE: 1"=10'-0"

CONTOUR LINES	NAME:	10-4

5. **Site Plans.** This assignment will be evaluated based on the following factors: accuracy of the property lines and symbols, neatness of work, and degree to which directions were followed. The assignment is to be presented on B-size paper (12″ × 18″). You will need two sheets. The drawing will be oriented with the long dimension horizontal. Identify the drawing as Drawing 10-5.

Directions. Locate point A 1-3/4″ from the top edge of the paper and 3-3/4″ from the left edge. This is the beginning property corner and is at the water's edge of Sandy Lake. Now locate the tip of the north arrow 2″ from the top edge and 2″ from the right edge. North has a bearing of 15° to the right of a vertical line. Draw the north symbol at the location described. Hint: Turn the drawing so that north points straight up.

Property Lines. Proceed to identify and draw the property boundary lines described below using a scale of 1″ = 20′-0″.
- Begin at point A.
- Line AB bears N 75° E for a distance of 200.0′.
- Line BC bears S 15° E for a distance of 112.0′.
- Line CD bears S 36° W for a distance of 70.0′.
- Line DE bears S 85° W for a distance of 154.0′.
- Determine the bearing and chord length of EA.

Point E is also on the water's edge of Sandy Lake. The lake shore roughly follows the contour lines provided for you on the elevation grid data chart on the back of this page. Label all corners (A, B, C, D, and E) and assign the following elevations to each corner.
- Elevation of A is 100.0′.
- Elevation of B is 106.4′.
- Elevation of C is 108.6′.
- Elevation of D is 107.9′.
- Elevation of E is 100.0′.

Elevation Grid. On another B-size sheet, lay out an elevation grid for the data shown on the elevation grid chart.

Grid lines are spaced 1/2″ apart or 10′-0″ at 1″ = 20′-0″ scale. Plot the contour lines at each one foot interval (101, 102, 103, etc.). Grid lines A-1 correspond to point A on the property line description. The 100.0′ contour line should also pass through corner E of the site. Hint: The property boundary lines should fall inside the contour grid. Once you have located the contour lines, trace them on the sheet that contains the property lines.

Foliage and Features. Locate the following trees on the site.
- Oak 30′ diameter. From E N 55° E 50.0′ to center of tree.
- Oak 20′ diameter. From A N 90° E 80.0′ to center of tree.
- Oak 20′ diameter. From B S 45° W 30.0′ to center of tree.
- Pine 15′ diameter. From C N 90° W 15.0′ to center of tree.

Add the following features:
- Sandy beach from water's edge to the 102.0′ elevation contour line.
- Lake name, lot #8, scale, title.
- Boat dock 3′ × 20′ with posts every 10′.
- For the dock, begin at the 101.0′ contour line anywhere along the beach.

Elevation Grid Data Chart for use with Problem/Activity 10-5

	A	B	C	D	E	F	G	H	I	J	K	L	M	N	O	P	Q	R	S	T	U
1	100.0	101.3	103.2	104.4	105.2	106.0	106.5	107.0	107.5	108.0	108.4	108.8	108.6	108.3	108.0	107.5	107.1	106.8	106.7	106.5	106.4
2	99.6	101.1	102.7	104.0	105.0	105.8	106.4	106.8	107.4	107.8	108.3	108.7	108.8	108.6	108.2	107.6	107.0	106.8	106.7	106.6	106.6
3	99.4	100.8	102.2	103.5	104.6	105.6	106.3	106.7	107.3	107.7	108.2	108.6	109.0	108.7	108.4	107.8	107.2	106.8	106.7	106.7	106.8
4	99.2	100.5	101.9	103.2	104.2	105.2	106.1	106.5	107.6	107.6	107.9	108.4	108.7	108.8	108.5	108.1	107.4	106.9	106.8	106.9	107.3
5	99.1	100.4	101.7	103.0	103.7	104.8	105.7	106.3	107.4	107.7	108.2	108.2	108.6	109.0	108.5	108.2	107.7	107.3	107.2	107.3	107.5
6	99.1	100.4	101.6	102.7	103.5	104.5	105.3	106.0	107.0	107.4	107.9	107.9	108.5	108.8	108.7	108.2	107.7	107.6	107.4	107.5	107.7
7	99.2	100.4	101.5	102.6	103.4	104.3	104.8	105.6	106.7	107.3	107.8	107.8	108.4	108.7	108.8	108.1	107.7	107.7	107.7	107.8	107.9
8	99.3	100.5	101.5	102.5	103.4	104.2	104.7	105.4	106.6	107.2	107.7	107.7	108.3	108.7	108.8	108.1	107.8	107.8	107.9	108.1	108.2
9	99.5	100.4	101.5	102.4	103.3	104.0	104.5	105.1	106.4	106.9	107.6	107.6	108.2	108.7	108.8	108.3	108.0	108.1	108.2	108.3	108.3
10	99.6	100.3	101.6	102.3	103.2	103.9	104.5	105.0	106.3	106.8	107.5	107.5	108.1	108.6	108.8	108.5	108.3	108.3	108.4	108.4	108.4
11	99.7	101.0	101.8	102.4	103.5	103.8	104.4	105.0	106.2	106.7	107.4	107.4	108.0	108.5	108.9	108.7	108.5	108.5	108.5	108.5	108.5
12	100.0	101.2	102.0	102.5	103.4	103.8	104.4	105.0	106.1	106.7	107.4	107.4	107.8	108.4	108.8	108.9	108.7	108.7	108.7	108.7	108.6
13	100.4	101.3	102.2	102.6	103.4	103.4	104.4	104.9	106.0	106.6	107.3	107.3	107.6	108.2	108.5	108.8	109.0	108.9	108.8	108.8	108.8
14	100.7	101.6	102.4	102.7	103.4	103.4	104.4	104.8	105.9	106.5	107.1	107.1	107.4	107.8	108.2	108.5	108.7	108.6	108.8	108.8	108.9
15	101.0	101.8	102.5	102.9	103.4	103.9	104.3	104.7	105.8	106.3	106.7	106.7	107.3	107.6	107.9	108.3	108.4	108.5	108.6	108.7	108.7
16						104.0	104.3	104.7	105.7	106.0	106.0	106.5	107.0	107.3	107.5	107.9	108.2	108.3	108.4	108.5	108.6

Explanation: The point where grid line "A" crosses grid line "1" is 100.0' elevation. The grid lines are drawn 1/2" apart or 10'-0" at the scale of 1"=20'-0". This is a chart of grid data and not the grid itself. You must draw the grid to scale and record the data on the grid before locating the contour lines.

6. **Plot Plans.** This assignment will be evaluated based on the following factors: proper placement of the house on the site; appropriate method of dimensioning the house on the site; correct size and location of drive, street, and utilities; neatness of work; and the degree to which directions were followed. The assignment is to be presented on B-size paper (12″ × 18″) using a standard border and title block. The drawing should be turned with the long edge horizontal. Identify the drawing as Drawing 10-6. Scale is 1″ = 20′-0″.

Directions. Using the site developed in Problem/Activity 10-5, draw a plot plan that has the following elements.

A. Trace the property lines, contour lines, trees, dock, etc., from Problem/Activity 10-5. Be sure to correct any errors that you made on the assignment.

B. Use the house and garage shown on the back of this page as the house to be located on the site.

C. The house is 53′-0″ across the front and the front should be parallel to the property line that has a bearing of S 15° E.

D. Draw the exterior walls (foundation only) and show them as 8″ or 12″ thick. Shade the wall thickness as though it were a single line. Omit windows, doors, and interior walls. Shade or hatch the interior space so the house space is highly visible on the plan.

E. Show the deck, porch between house and garage, and steps on the plot plan. Show the boards.

F. Locate the following features outside the property lines: gas line, water, sewer, edge of street, and centerline of street. Each of these items is dimensioned to the lot line that is parallel to the street. Use these dimensions:
   - Gas line: 8′-0″
   - Water line: 18′-0″
   - Sewer line: 26′-0″
   - Edge of street: 20′-6″
   - Center of street: 33′-0″

G. Lay out a paved drive 20′-0″ wide at the garage, but 10′-0″ at the street. Provide a turnaround using proper turning radii. Refer to Problem/Activity 9-6.

H. Dimension the following:
   - Reference corner of house location.
   - Location of all utilities to the property line.
   - Drive dimensions and centers of all radii. Show tangent points.

I. Label the following:
   - Elevation of house reference corner.
   - Drive.
   - Street name of your choice.
   - Include everything from the site plan from Problem/Activity 10-5.

J. Complete the drawing by adding the scale and title.

Floor plan for use with Problem/Activity 10-6

Scale: 1"=10'-0"

Footings, Foundations, and Concrete

11

Text, Pages 233–258

Name _____

Course _____ Date _____ Score _____

Part I: Completion
Complete each sentence with the proper response. Place your answer on the space provided.

1. When staking out the house location, a surveyor's transit must be used for measuring angles other than _____ degrees.

1. _____

2. The distances used to locate the corners of the house are taken from the _____ plan.

2. _____

3. To lay out square corners, the 9-12-_____ unit method can be used.

3. _____

4. _____ measurements check the position of the corners for accuracy (squareness).

4. _____

5. The location of the foundation is kept during excavation and construction by the use of _____.

5. _____

6. Batter boards are placed approximately _____ outside the footing line.

6. _____

7. To ensure that each stake of the batter boards is placed accurately, a _____ is used.

7. _____

8. The corner having the highest elevation is normally selected for the _____ point.

8. _____

9. The finished floor of the house should be a minimum of _____ above the grade.

9. _____

10. Footings should be excavated at least _____ into undisturbed earth and a minimum of 6″ below the average maximum frost penetration depth.

10. _____

11. To obtain the minimum footing depth for any given area, check the local _____.

11. _____

12. Where part of the footings bear on rock, remove approximately _____ of the rock and replace with compacted sand to equalize settling.

12. _____

13. Only when soil tests prove that the earth is adequately compacted to sustain a building should _____ be placed in filled or regraded soils.

13. _____

14. Excavate a gentle back slope in _____ soil.

15. Excavation in _____ permits a steep slope.

16. Beams may be either metal or _____.

17. The _____ (top/bottom) flange on a steel post is larger.

18. Lintels should extend at least _____ into a masonry wall on either side of an opening.

19. Sidewalks, driveways, footings, and basement floors require one part cement, _____ part(s) sand, and five parts aggregate.

20. Vibrating or _____ poured concrete results in a more dense product and dislodges weak spots caused by air pockets.

21. A _____ wide flange beam (less than 16″ deep) is the most economical (lightest) for supporting a uniform load of 55 kips (55,000 lbs.) that spans 14′. Refer to the chart in your text.

14. _____

15. _____

16. _____

17. _____

18. _____

19. _____

20. _____

21. _____

Part II: Short Answer/Listing
Provide brief answers to the following questions.

1. What is the purpose of a footing? _____
_____
_____

2. What material is normally used for the footings of residential structures? _____
_____

3. Generally, how thick and wide should the footing be? _____
_____
_____
_____

4. Why might a difference in settling occur for a structure resting on two different subsoils?
_____
_____

5. What can be done to footings to reduce cracks caused by uneven settling? Remember that the weight of most residential structures lies on two rather than all four walls. _____
_____
_____

6. When would longitudinal reinforcing bars be used in footings? _____
_____
_____

Name _____

7. How thick should the footing be for a fireplace? _____

8. What can be done to prevent cracking where steps are located in horizontal and vertical footings? _____

_____

_____

9. Where do the foundation walls begin and terminate on a residential structure? _____

_____

_____

10. Name common materials used to construct foundation walls. _____

_____

_____

_____

11. Name the four basic types of foundation walls. _____

_____

_____

_____

12. What factors determine the type of foundation to be used? _____

_____

_____

_____

13. What are form boards and when are they used? _____

_____

_____

_____

14. Should the foundation wall of a slab foundation extend below the frost line? _____

15. Name three advantages of a slab foundation. _____

_____

_____

_____

16. Give three reasons why built-up wood beams are used more often than solid wood beams in residential construction. _____

_____

_____

_____

17. Name two characteristics of solid wood beams. _____

_____

18. Which has greater strength, the S-beam or the W-beam? _____

19. What are live loads? Give some examples. _____

_____

_____

_____

20. Define dead loads. Give some examples. _____

_____

_____

_____

21. List four materials from which lintels are commonly made. _____

_____

_____

_____

22. List three places where contraction joints should be located. _____

_____

_____

23. Identify the type of foundation shown in the following drawings.

A. _____

B. _____

C. _____

D. _____

E. _____

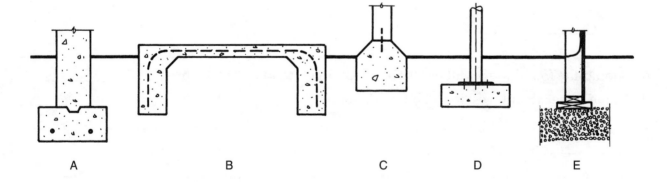

A   B   C   D   E

24. Identify the drain tile, sill, header, and expansion joint on the following basement wall drawing.

A. _____

B. _____

C. _____

D. _____

A

B

2 × 10 JOIST

7–5

D

C

8"

1–4

Part III: Multiple Choice

Select the best answer and write the corresponding letter in the space provided.

1. The posts used in post foundations are commonly made of:

   1. _____

   A. Masonry.
   B. Steel.
   C. Pressure-treated wood.
   D. All of the above.

2. A wood foundation is particularly suitable in:

   2. _____

   A. A garage where the distance is too great to span with floor joists.
   B. Areas where the sea level is high.
   C. Warmer climates where freezing of the ground is infrequent.
   D. None of the above.

3. For a wood foundation, the trench excavated for a structure with a crawl space should be _____ deep.

   A. less than 10"
   B. at least 12"
   C. 9"
   D. 6"

3. _____

4. When using a wood foundation for a basement:

   A. The site is excavated 12" deeper than the regular depth.
   B. A basement sump is installed in poorly drained soils.
   C. No foundation drainage is necessary.
   D. All of the above.

4. _____

5. Nails used in wood foundations should be made of:

   A. Hot-dipped zinc-coated steel.
   B. Copper.
   C. Silicon bronze.
   D. All of the above.

5. _____

6. The floor joists or trusses of a wood foundation are placed on the:

   A. Double top plate of the foundation wall.
   B. Inside of the foundation wall.
   C. Basement floor slab.
   D. None of the above.

6. _____

7. Backfilling for a wood foundation should be started:

   A. Before the floor joists or trusses are installed.
   B. Before the polyethylene film is applied.
   C. After the basement floor has cured and the first floor is installed.
   D. All of the above.

7. _____

8. The factor(s) that determine(s) the ability of a concrete or masonry basement wall to resist earth pressure include:

   A. Support from crosswalls.
   B. The size of the floor joists.
   C. The live load of the structure.
   D. All of the above.

8. _____

9. The distance from the top of the basement floor to the bottom of the floor joists above should be no less than:

   A. 5'
   B. 6'
   C. 7'
   D. 8'

9. _____

10. Basement load bearing crosswalls should be attached to exterior walls by:

    A. Metal tie bars.
    B. A masonry bond.
    C. Anchor bolts.
    D. All of the above.

10. _____

11. If the wood sill bears on the outer and inner face shells of a block foundation wall:

    A. Cap the top course of block using 4″ solid block.
    B. Capping may be omitted.
    C. Cores in the top course are filled with concrete or mortar.
    D. The top course may be capped with reinforced concrete masonry bond beam.

11. _____

12. Concrete block basement walls should be damp-proofed to eliminate ground water from seeping through the wall. This is done by:

    A. Painting the outside of the blocks with oil base paints.
    B. Applying a 1/4″ coat of fire clay.
    C. Applying two 1/4″ thick coats of cement-mortar or plaster then a coat of hot tar or a similar water-proofing material.
    D. All of the above.

12. _____

13. To eliminate water damage to basements in wet or poorly drained soils:

    A. Install a check valve in the floor drain to keep water from flowing in through the drain.
    B. Reinforce the floor slab to resist uplift from groundwater pressure.
    C. Install a sump pump to take away any water that seeps in.
    D. All of the above.

13. _____

14. To support a 4″ masonry wall above an opening, the smallest piece of steel angle that can be used for a 10′-6″ span is _____. Refer to Figure 11-38 in the textbook.

    A. 3-1/2″ × 3-1/2″ × 5/16″
    B. 4″ × 4″ × 5/16″
    C. 4″ × 4″ × 3/8″
    D. 6″ × 4″ × 3/8″

14. _____

15. A float is used in finishing concrete to:

    A. Embed the large aggregate just beneath the surface.

    B. Remove any slight imperfections, lumps, and voids to produce a flat surface.

    C. Consolidate mortar at the surface in preparation for final steel-troweling.

    D. All of the above.

15. _____

16. When ordering concrete, allow _____ cubic feet to the yard.

    A. 24

    B. 25

    C. 26

    D. 27

16. _____

17. Concrete slabs are normally placed on a base of compacted sand _____ thick.

    A. 4″ to 6″

    B. 5″ to 7″

    C. 6″ to 8″

    D. 9″ to 10″

17. _____

18. The actual size of a typical "concrete block" (hollow concrete masonry unit) is _____.

    A. 7-5/8″ × 7-5/8″ × 15-5/8″

    B. 8″ × 8″ × 16″

    C. 8-5/8″ × 8-5/8″ × 16-5/8″

    D. 9″ × 9″ × 18″

18. _____

Name _____

Part IV: Matching
Match the correct term with its description listed below. Place the corresponding letter on the space provided.

A. ACA or CCA
B. Aggregate
C. AWWF
D. Bearing wall
E. Cement
F. Concrete
G. Contraction joint
H. Float
I. Jointing tool
J. Kip

K. Lintel
L. PWF
M. Pier foundation
N. Plot plan
O. S-beam
P. Saw kerf
Q. Screed
R. Slab foundation
S. T-foundation
T. Trowel

1. Provides the dimensions to be used when staking out the location of the house on the lot.

1. _____

2. Prevents movement of string along batter board.

2. _____

3. The name of this foundation comes from its shape.

3. _____

4. Sometimes called a thickened-edge slab.

4. _____

5. A foundation used in a crawl space where the distance is too large for a single span.

5. _____

6. Permanent wood foundation.

6. _____

7. All weather wood foundation.

7. _____

8. Waterborne preservative salts.

8. _____

9. Supports a portion of the load of the building.

9. _____

10. Formerly called an I-beam.

10. _____

11. Equals 1,000 pounds.

11. _____

12. A horizontal structural element that supports the load over openings such as windows or doors.

12. _____

13. The combination of cement, sand, aggregate, and water.

13. _____

14. Contains lime, silica, alumina, iron components, and gypsum.

14. _____

15. Stone or gravel.

15. _____

16. Used to smooth a concrete surface.

16. _____

17. A foot long board with a handle attached to one of the flat sides.

17. _____

18. A concrete finishing tool used in a circular motion to further harden the surface and develop a very smooth finish.

18. _____

19. Used in large areas of concrete to control cracking.

19. _____

20. Used to cut grooves in freshly placed concrete.

20. _____

Part V: Problems/Activities

1.

Directions:
Draw a typical foundation wall section for a thickened-edge slab that includes the following elements:

> Scale: 3/4" = 1'-0"
> Foundation 10" thick and 48" from top of slab to bottom of foundation (no footing). Thickness and depth should conform to code.
> Welded wire fabric in foundation and slab.
> Slab 4" thick on 1" RF insulation and 4" compacted sand.
> Wall on foundation of 8" concrete block with 3/4" RF insulation outside extending 24" below the grade. Use wood siding over insulation to 2" above the grade. Flash exposed insulation with aluminum.
> Label and dimension. Add scale.

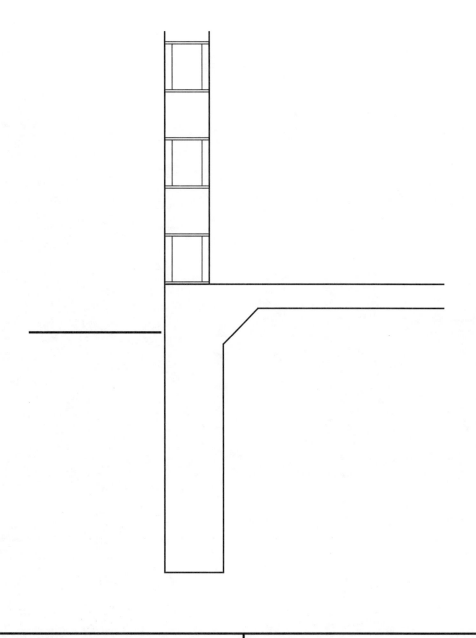

SLAB FOUNDATION SECTION	NAME:	11-1

2.

Directions:
Draw a typical foundation wall section for a frame structure with siding that has a crawl space.
Include the following elements in your drawing:
> Scale: 3/4" = 1'-0"
> Continuous footing 8" × 16" with 2-1/2" rebar and 4" perforated drain tile in pea gravel.
> 8" concrete block foundation wall (6 courses high or code) with 1/2" parge coat for moisture
  protection. Grade 8" below top of foundation and crawl space from top of footing to bottom
  of joists.
> 2" × 8" treated sill plate with 1/2" × 16" anchor bolts and sill sealer.
> 2" × 10" floor joist with 3/4" T&G P.W. glued and nailed.
> Frame wall with 3/4" RF insulation to top of foundation with horizontal siding, 3-1/2" batt
  insulation, and 1/2" drywall.
> Label and dimension. Add scale.

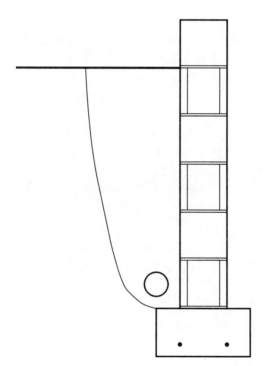

| FOUNDATION WITH CRAWL SPACE | NAME: | 11-2 |

3.

Directions:

Draw a typical foundation/basement wall section for a brick veneer on a frame residential structure. Include the following elements in your drawing:

> Scale: 3/4" = 1'-0"
> Continuous footing 12" × 24" with 2-1/2" rebar and 4" perforated drain tile in pea gravel.
> 12" thick basement wall with 4" brick ledge and damp-proofing. Basement floor to ceiling should be 7'-10" to 8'-0".
> 4" basement floor slab with welded wire fabric and 4" compacted sand with vapor barrier.
> 2" × 8" treated sill plate with sill sealer and 1/2" × 8" anchor bolts.
> Floor system is 14" wood floor trusses to span 24'-0" with 3/4" T&G P.W. panels glued and nailed. See Reference Section in text.
> First floor frame wall has 3/4" RF insulation, 3-1/2" batt insulation, and 1/2" drywall inside. Veneer is common brick with 1" air space, wall ties, and flashing.
> Label and dimension. Add scale.

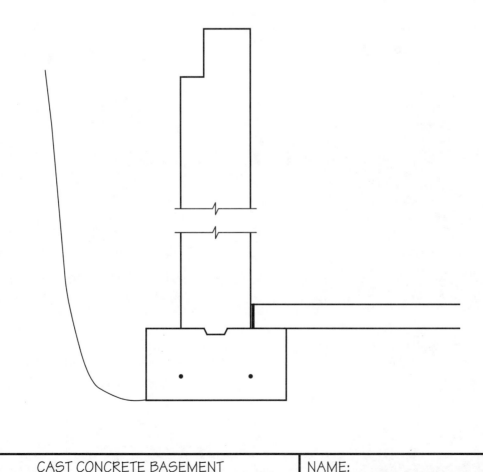

| CAST CONCRETE BASEMENT | NAME: | 11-3 |

4.

Directions:

Draw a typical foundation/basement wall section for a residential structure that requires a wood foundation. Include the following elements:

> Scale: 3/4″ = 1′-0″
> Base for foundation is 8″ of crushed stone or gravel.
> Foundation/basement wall is 2″ × 6″ frame with 2″ × 10″ footing plate and 3/4″ P.W. sheathing covered with polyethylene film. All wood materials are specially treated for this application.
> Include protection strip at grade, double top plate, and 1″ × 4″ screed.
> Basement floor is 4″ thick with welded wire fabric and moisture barrier. Include drain tiles where ground water is a problem.
> First floor system is 2″ × 10″ joists with 3/4″ T&G P.W. glued and nailed.
> Exterior wall is 2″ × 4″ stud, 3/4″ RF insulation, siding, and 1/2″ drywall.
> Label and dimension. Add scale.

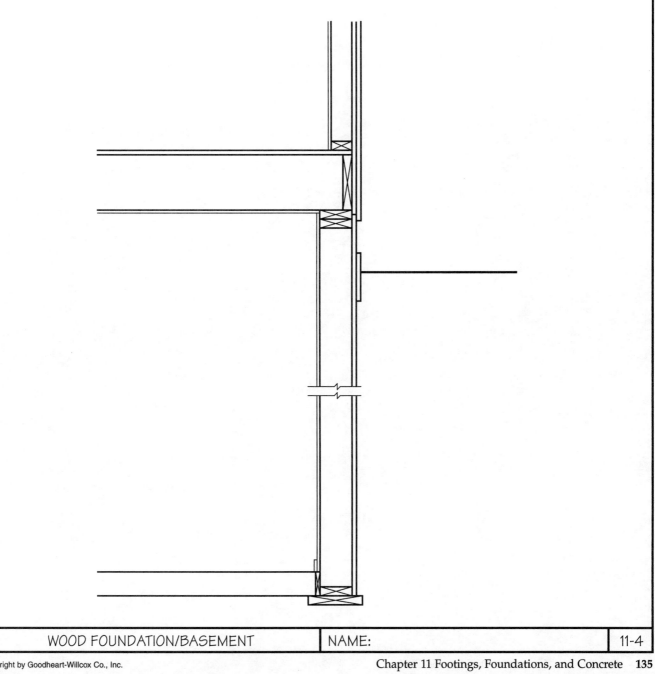

WOOD FOUNDATION/BASEMENT	NAME:	11-4

The Foundation Plan

12

Text, Pages 259–271

Name _____

Course _____ Date _____ Score _____

Part I: Short Answer/Listing
Provide brief answers to the following questions.

1. From which three sources of information is the foundation plan drawn? _____

   _____

   _____

   _____

2. Name five things a foundation plan usually includes. _____

   _____

   _____

   _____

   _____

3. Why should you examine the floor plan to determine the type of exterior walls before drawing the foundation plan? _____

   _____

   _____

   _____

4. What is the first step in drawing a foundation plan? _____

   _____

5. The basement plan is a combination of two plans. Name the two plans. _____

   _____

6. Identify the material symbols used on foundation plans.

A. _____

B. _____

C. _____

D. _____

E. _____

F. _____

G. _____

H. _____

I. _____

J. _____

K. _____

L. _____

M. _____

N. _____

O. _____

7. Why is it good practice to use the preliminary floor plan as an underlay for drawing the foundation plan? _____

_____

_____

8. A beam generally is represented by which of the following linetypes (symbols)? Circle the letter.

A. ———————————————————————

B. ——————— — — ——————— — — ———————

C. ——————— — —————— — ——————— — — ———————

D. None of the above.

9. How are pier locations dimensioned? _____

Name _____

10. How does a basement/foundation plan differ from a foundation plan? _____

_____

_____

_____

11. What is the final step when drawing a foundation plan or basement plan? _____

_____

_____

12. When is it necessary to show electrical switches, outlets, and fixtures on a basement plan?

_____

_____

Part II: Completion

Complete each sentence with the proper response. Place your answer on the space provided.

1. A _____ house is a good example of a house style that requires both a foundation plan and a basement plan.

1. _____

2. The foundation plan shows the location and size of footings, piers, _____, foundation walls, and supporting beams.

2. _____

3. The foundation plan is prepared primarily for excavators, _____, carpenters, and cement workers who build the foundation.

3. _____

4. Houses in cold climates usually have _____ because the footings must be below the frost line, which may be several feet deep.

4. _____

5. The foundation plan is usually drawn after the _____ plan and elevations have been roughed out.

5. _____

6. The scale most commonly used in residential drawings is _____.

6. _____

7. The _____ linetype (symbol) is used for drawing the footings for foundation walls.

7. _____

8. Interior frame walls should be dimensioned to their _____ on a basement/foundation plan.

8. _____

9. Openings in a masonry wall are dimensioned to the _____ of the opening.

9. _____

10. Study the elevation and _____ plan to determine if retaining walls, stepped footings, or other grade considerations are needed.

10. _____

11. Considering the cost per square foot, a basement costs much _____ than the first floor.

11. _____

Part III: Multiple Choice

Select the best answer and write the corresponding letter in the space provided.

1. Ms. Smith and Mr. Jones are each building a house from the same floor plan. Ms. Smith is using a stud wall with siding and Mr. Jones is using brick veneer. Which of the following statements is true?

    A. The size of the foundations will be exactly the same.

    B. Mr. Jones's foundation will be 8″ longer and wider than Ms. Smith's because a brick veneer house needs a 4″ ledge on all four sides.

    C. Ms. Smith's foundation plan will be 4″ longer and wider than Mr. Jones's because a stud wall requires a 4″ ledge on the length and width.

    D. None of the above statements apply.

1. _____

2. Prior to drawing the foundation plan, you should:

    A. Study available information to make a decision about the size of the footings and foundation walls.

    B. Determine the frost penetration depth for the area where the dwelling will be built.

    C. Check with local building codes to be sure that the requirements will be met.

    D. All of the above.

2. _____

3. Which of the following is a difference when drawing a foundation or basement plan with CADD as compared to manual drafting?

    A. The drawing is created at full scale.

    B. The floor plan is not used.

    C. Dimensions are not needed as the drawing is so accurate it can be scaled.

    D. There are no differences.

3. _____

4. What is the last step when drawing a foundation or basement plan using CADD?

    A. Add text to the drawing.

    B. Add the title of the drawing.

    C. Determine the plot scale.

    D. Look over the plan to be sure it is complete.

4. _____

Name _____

Part IV: Matching
Match the correct term with its description listed below. Place the corresponding letter on the space provided.

A. Dwarf walls.
B. Concrete block symbol.
C. Foundation details.

D. Material symbols.
E. Soil bearing test.
F. Windows or doors.

1. Verifies the load bearing capacity of the soil.

1. _____

2. Describes the foundation structure.

2. _____

3. Used on drawings to represent various building materials.

3. _____

4. Low walls constructed to retain an embankment or excavation.

4. _____

5. Openings in the foundation wall.

5. _____

6. Used on a drawing to shade concrete block foundation walls.

6. _____

1.

Directions:
Use the floor plan of the garden house below to construct a thickened-edge slab foundation in the space provided. Scale is 1/4″ = 1′-0″. Include the following elements in your drawing:

> Thickness of foundation wall (8″) and slab floor (4″).
> Anchor bolts (1/2″ × 8″) at least every 4 feet along perimeter.
> Cutting plane through one foundation wall. Draw the section and dimension it. Foundation depth should be at least 24″ or frost depth for your area.

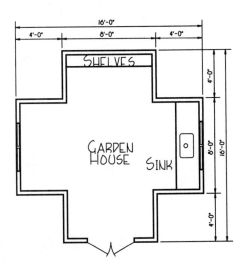

FLOOR PLAN
SCALE: 1/8″ = 1′-0″

| FOUNDATION PLAN | NAME: | 12-1 |

2.

Activity 12-2

Factors to be considered in the evaluation of this assignment include form and style of your work, accuracy of the solution, elements identified properly, and accepted construction technology represented.

Directions:

Study Chapter 12 in your text before starting this assignment. You will need a sheet of C-size (18" × 24") paper for this assignment. Using the floor plan provided below, construct a basement/foundation plan at 1/4" = 1'-0" scale that includes the following features:

> Show footings for the foundation walls and pier.
> Use 12" concrete block, 8" concrete block with pilasters, or 10" cast concrete foundation walls.
> Include stairs and all interior walls in the basement. You decide on the arrangement and use of space.
> Show all openings in the foundation walls and provide several basement windows and walkout to a patio to the rear of the house.
> Indicate floor joist direction, spacing, and size.
> Provide a floor drain and sump near the washer.
> Locate the water storage tank, water heater, washer, dryer, furnace, and electrical distribution panel in the basement.
> Add material symbols, dimensions, scale, and title block.
> Show a cutting-plane line to indicate a typical wall section detail.

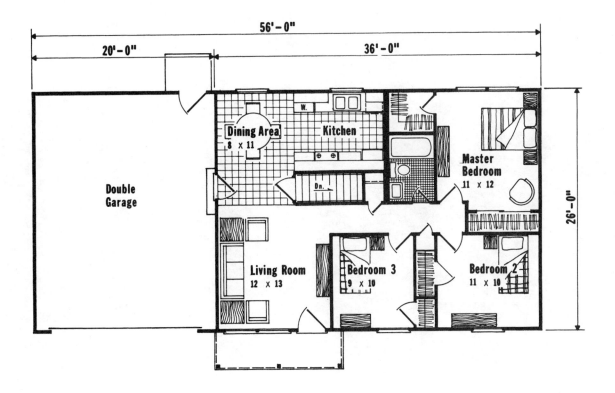

Sill and Floor Construction
13

Text, Pages 273–296

Name _____

Course _____ Date _____ Score _____

Part I: Short Answer/Listing
Provide brief answers to the following questions.

1. Name the structural members that are used in both platform and balloon framing. _____

   _____

   _____

2. List three reasons why platform framing is popular. _____

   _____

   _____

   _____

3. When using platform framing to construct a floor, what is the starting point? _____

   _____

4. What members provide support for the flooring? _____

   _____

5. Double joist framing is required to accommodate large openings in the floor. Give two examples of typical openings. _____

   _____

6. Name two disadvantages of balloon framing. _____

   _____

   _____

7. What feature of balloon framing makes it unique? _____

   _____

   _____

8. List the two types of sill construction used in balloon framing. _____

   _____

   _____

9. Name the four factors that determine the joist sizes chosen for a particular area of the structure. _____

_____

_____

_____

10. Using the chart in the text, determine the allowable span for a 2″ × 12″ joist when the following conditions are present: The load is 30 pounds per square foot, the species is southern yellow pine, the grade is Number 2 dense, and the spacing is 16″OC. _____

_____

11. Name two reasons why panel products are often used as subfloor materials. _____

_____

_____

12. Subflooring panels 1/2″ or 5/8″ thick are used when the joists are placed 16″OC. List the types of panel products that may be used. _____

_____

_____

13. Name two techniques used in residential construction to provide the required support for floors with heavy loads. _____

_____

_____

14. In post and beam construction, 2″ decking is commonly used. In general, what is the maximum allowable span for the beams? _____

_____

15. Two types of foundations are possible for post and beam construction. Name both.

_____

_____

16. Identify the size beam needed in the following situation. Refer to the chart in the text. The designer has specified a glue-laminated roof beam to span 24′-0″, the dead load is expected to be 8 pounds per square foot, the live load is estimated to be 20 pounds per square foot, and the beam spacing is 10′. _____

_____

Name _____

17. Label the drawings of the various beams used in post and beam construction.

A. _____
B. _____
C. _____
D. _____
E. _____

A   B   C   D   E

18. Name two types of wood from which joists are usually made. _____

_____

19. Name four advantages of engineered wood floor trusses. _____

_____

_____

_____

20. What is the single greatest disadvantage for engineered wood products (EWPs) as a group?

_____

21. What is the main difference between plywood and laminated veneer lumber (LVL)? _____

_____

_____

Part II: Completion
Complete each sentence with the proper response. Place your answer on the space provided.

1. In the longitudinal system of beam placement in post and beam construction, the beams are placed at _____ to the roof slope.

1. _____

2. Curtain _____ construction allows wide expanses of glass without the need for headers.

2. _____

3. Cross bridging is used to stiffen the _____ and spread the load over a broader area in typical floor joist construction.

3. _____

4. In platform framing, a method called _____ sill construction is used.

4. _____

5. In T-sill construction, a _____ is placed inside the stud perimeter.

5. _____

6. The actual (dry) size of a 2″ × 10″ floor joist is _____.

6. _____

7. The framing member that is nailed to the ends of the floor joists is called a _____.

7. _____

8. When a floor area is to be cantilevered 2′ beyond a foundation wall, the joists should extend inside _____ for adequate support.

8. _____

9. In T-sill construction, the studs are nailed to the sill plate and the _____.

9. _____

10. Advantages of balloon framing include little shrinkage and _____ stability.

10. _____

11. The size of a nominal 1″ × 6″ board is _____ when dry.

11. _____

12. A floor that uses girders or _____ requires fewer support members.

12. _____

13. Load-bearing walls may be made from concrete block, cast concrete, or _____ construction.

13. _____

14. Use _____ between the joists when the space between the joists is used as a cold air return duct.

14. _____

15. Floor trusses are made of _____-graded lumber to minimize the amount of material used.

15. _____

16. Engineered wood floor trusses are commonly made from _____ or 2″ × 6″ lumber.

16. _____

17. Subfloor panels must be _____ along all edges.

17. _____

18. In some areas of the country, the subfloor and _____ are combined into a single thickness.

18. _____

19. Subfloor panels should have some space between them to allow for _____.

19. _____

20. In post and beam construction, wide overhangs may be provided by lengthening the large _____.

20. _____

21. Roof and floor decking planks generally range in thickness from 2″ to _____.

21. _____

22. Insulation for roof planking is placed between the _____ and roof material.

22. _____

Name _____

Part III: Multiple Choice
Select the best answer and write the corresponding letter in the space provided.

1. Actual dimensions of sills used in most residential construction are:

    A. 1-1/2″ × 5-1/2″
    B. 2″ × 6″
    C. 2-1/2″ × 6-1/2″
    D. 3″ × 7″

    1. _____

2. Which of the following statements is true of solid sill construction?

    A. Studs are nailed to the sill plate and the header.
    B. Headers are not required.
    C. A fire-stop is unnecessary.
    D. All of the above.

    2. _____

3. In residential construction, floor joists are usually spaced _____ OC.

    A. 12″
    B. 14″
    C. 16″
    D. 18″

    3. _____

4. A beam used to reduce the span of joists may be _____.

    A. a metal S-beam
    B. a solid timber
    C. built-up from dimensional lumber
    D. All of the above.

    4. _____

5. Engineered wood floor trusses are commonly spaced _____ OC.

    A. 12″
    B. 18″
    C. 24″
    D. 30″

    5. _____

6. Gluing and nailing 5/8″ subfloor panels to 2″ × 8″ joists increases stiffness by approximately _____ percent.

    A. 25
    B. 40
    C. 55
    D. 70

    6. _____

7. The concrete base for tile or stone supported by wood floor joists should _____.

    A. be reinforced with wire mesh
    B. have a layer of building paper under the concrete
    C. use a special type of concrete
    D. All of the above.

    7. _____

8. In post and beam construction, most of the weight is carried by the _____.

8. _____

    A. beams
    B. headers
    C. posts
    D. curtain wall

9. In post and beam construction, the size of the footings is determined by the _____.

9. _____

    A. width of the building
    B. soil bearing capacity
    C. type of curtain wall used
    D. All of the above.

Part IV: Matching

Match the correct term with its description listed below. Place the corresponding letter on the space provided.

    A. A special type of concrete
    B. Built-in camber
    C. Cantilevered joists
    D. Engineered wood floor trusses

    E. Metal plates
    F. Post and beam construction
    G. Transverse method

1. Provide clear spans with a minimum of depth in a lightweight assembly.

1. _____

2. Assures that the chords of the floor trusses will be level when loaded.

2. _____

3. Used when a portion of the floor extends outside the foundation wall.

3. _____

4. Provides a base for ceramic tile, stone, and slate floors.

4. _____

5. Provides greater spans and more flexibility in design.

5. _____

6. Used in post and beam construction when the beams follow the roof slope and decking runs parallel to the roof ridge.

6. _____

7. Used to connect large beam segments.

7. _____

Part V: Problems/Activities

1.

Directions:
Using guidelines and proper form, label and dimension the basement wall section below using the following information:

> Footing is 12" × 24" with two 1/2" rebars and drain tile in pea gravel.
> Basement floor is 4" thick with a 4" sand base and 3/8" expansion joint.
> Basement wall is 12" concrete block with a 1/2" parge coat outside.
> Distance from the top of the footing to grade (224.2' elevation) is 8'-8".
> Distance from the floor to the underside of 24" trusses is 8'-2".
> Anchor bolts are 1/2" × 16" spaced 8'-0" apart.
> Flooring material on the first floor is 3/4" T&G P.W.
> Stud wall is covered with 3/4" RF insulation and panel siding.

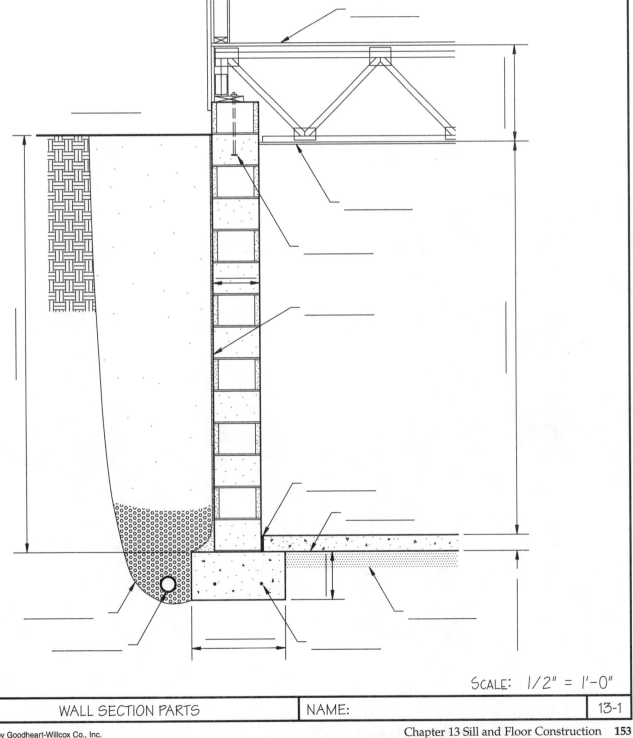

SCALE: 1/2" = 1'-0"

WALL SECTION PARTS	NAME:	13-1

2.

Directions:
Complete the floor framing problems below as indicated.
A. Draw the framing to allow for an opening 40″ × 36″ centered in the floor area. The shortest dimension is parallel to the joist direction. Use double headers and double trimmers. Dimension the opening and label the joists.
B. Plan the joist layout (16″ OC) for the area between existing joists and 2′ beyond the foundation wall. Label parts and show the dimensions.

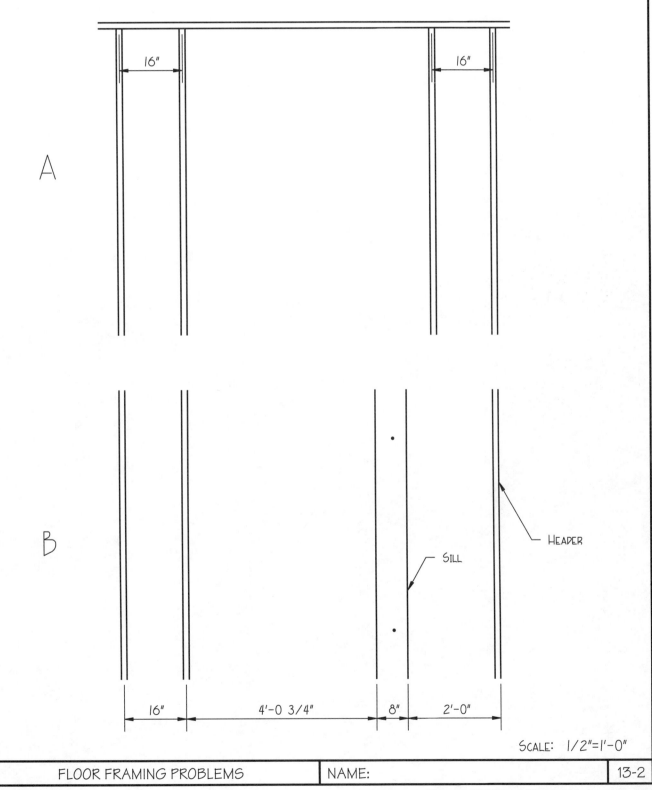

A

16″   16″

B

HEADER

SILL

16″   4′-0 3/4″   8″   2′-0″

SCALE: 1/2″=1′-0″

FLOOR FRAMING PROBLEMS   NAME: 13-2

3. **Floor Framing Plan.** This assignment will be evaluated based on the following factors: The quality of work, use of proper construction techniques, use of appropriate sizes for building materials for spans and economy, and overall communication.

Directions. You are to draw a floor framing plan and a typical section for the house shown in Figure 12-14 in your text. The scale should be 1/4″ = 1′-0″. Use C-size paper and center the drawing on the sheet. Include the following elements in your drawing:

- Use typical #2 Douglas fir floor framing materials (2″ × 8″, 2″ × 10″, 2″ × 12″) for sills and floor joists and standard 3/4″ tongue-and-groove plywood (4′ × 8′) for the floor material.
- Use platform framing and box sill construction.
- The basement is 10″ cast concrete and covers the space under the living area of the house except the garage. The garage has a 4″ thick floating slab floor.
- A steel beam is planned for the length of the house to support the joists. The total floor load is 50 pounds per square foot.
- The floor framing should allow space for 3/4″ rigid foam insulation sheathing on top of the foundation wall. Wood siding will form the exterior skin of the structure.
- Draw a typical section of the foundation wall between the garage and utility storage showing floor levels and construction. The garage floor should be 4″ above the grade line. Draw the section at 1/2″ = 1′-0″ scale.
- The sandstone hearth is to be supported on the floor.
- Add dimensions and notes necessary to build the floor framing.

Text, Pages 297–318

Name _____

Course _____ Date _____ Score _____

Part I: Matching
Match the correct term with its description listed below. Place the corresponding letter on the space provided.

A. Ashlar stonework

B. Ceiling joists

C. Common brick

D. Cripples

E. Flashing

F. Rubble stonework

G. Sole plate

H. Subfloor

I. Trimmers

J. Stucco

K. Veneer

1. Framing member used in residential frame wall construction.

1. _____

2. Provides a work surface for the construction of the frame walls.

2. _____

3. Studs that are not full length used above and below wall openings.

3. _____

4. Studs used in wall openings to support the header.

4. _____

5. Placed across the width of the structure after the top plates have been added.

5. _____

6. Composed of dressed, cut, or squared stones.

6. _____

7. Composed of irregularly shaped field stones.

7. _____

8. Facing material used in wall construction.

8. _____

9. Prevents moisture from entering solid masonry or brick veneer walls and behind the stucco shell.

9. _____

10. May have a lip on one or more edges.

10. _____

11. A coating applied to the outside of the structure.

11. _____

Part II: Multiple Choice
Select the best answer and write the corresponding letter in the space provided.

1. Which of the following species is generally used in wall framing lumber?

   A. Southern yellow pine
   B. Redwood
   C. Oak
   D. All of the above.

1. _____

2. Frame wall construction begins with the _____.

   A. header
   B. sole plate
   C. top plate
   D. studs

2. _____

3. A nailing edge for interior wall materials may be provided by which of the following?

   A. Fastening a 2″ × 6″ to cross blocking.
   B. Placing 1/2″ plywood sheathing next to the studs.
   C. Applying rigid foam insulation to the wall section.
   D. All of the above.

3. _____

4. Header size refers to which of the following?

   A. The overall size of the header.
   B. The size of the material used.
   C. The size of the rough opening plus the size of the spacer.
   D. None of the above.

4. _____

5. Trussed headers are more functional for _____.

   A. frame walls without corner bracing
   B. areas subject to high winds
   C. openings wider than 8′-0″
   D. All of the above.

5. _____

6. Special framing is needed for _____.

   A. extra bathtub support
   B. wall openings for heating ducts
   C. wall backing for a water closet
   D. All of the above.

6. _____

7. Which of the following statements is true of masonry veneer?

   A. Moisture does not collect between the veneer and the frame wall.
   B. The veneer does not support the weight of the wall.
   C. The most common thickness used is 1″.
   D. None of the above.

7. _____

8. A building material that has sharp corners and lines and is very uniform in size is _____.

    A. face brick
    B. common brick
    C. cobweb stone
    D. None of the above.

Part III: Completion

Complete each sentence with the proper response. Place your answer on the space provided.

1. The trend in residential frame wall construction is toward more _____ and less onsite construction.

    1. _____

2. The most common lumber grade is _____ grade.

    2. _____

3. The sole plate functions as an anchor for the wall and a _____ for interior and exterior wall sheathing.

    3. _____

4. A space of 8'-1 1/2" from the bottom of the ceiling joists to the top of the subfloor allows a finished wall height of approximately _____.

    4. _____

5. Construction time is _____ when using solid blocking.

    5. _____

6. The distance is usually the same from the top of each window and door to the _____.

    6. _____

7. All wall openings need a _____ or lintel above the opening to provide support for the weight above.

    7. _____

8. To prevent the ceiling joists from interfering with the roof slope, the upper corner of the joist is cut to match the _____ of the roof.

    8. _____

9. Framing around a ceiling opening for a disappearing stairway requires the use of _____ headers.

    9. _____

10. To provide support for a bay window when the unit is at right angles to the floor joists, _____ joists should be used.

    10. _____

11. Corrugated metal wall ties may be placed in mortar joints no farther apart than 16" vertically and _____ horizontally for bonding purposes.

    11. _____

12. One inch of dead air space should be left between masonry veneer and the _____ wall.

    12. _____

13. Termite _____ are placed at the base of solid masonry or brick veneers to prevent the entrance of termites.

    13. _____

14. The expected life span of a quality three-coat stucco surface can exceed _____ years.

    14. _____

Part IV: Short Answer/Listing

Provide brief answers to the following questions.

1. List the three types of residential wall construction. _____
   _____
   _____

2. Name the three types of bracing commonly used in frame wall construction. _____
   _____
   _____

3. Why would the exterior frame wall be placed 1/2″ to 3/4″ in from the outside edge of the foundation wall? _____
   _____

4. Is greater shrinkage more likely to occur in solid blocking construction or cripple construction? _____
   _____

5. In frame wall construction, the header is usually longer than the rough opening. Explain why.
   _____
   _____
   _____

6. How does ceiling joist construction differ from floor joist construction? _____
   _____
   _____

7. List the advantages and disadvantages of concrete block walls. _____
   _____
   _____
   _____
   _____

8. What are the advantages of a brick or stone veneer wall over a solid masonry wall? _____
   _____
   _____

9. Identify the brick bonds shown below.

A. _____

B. _____

C. _____

D. _____

A

B

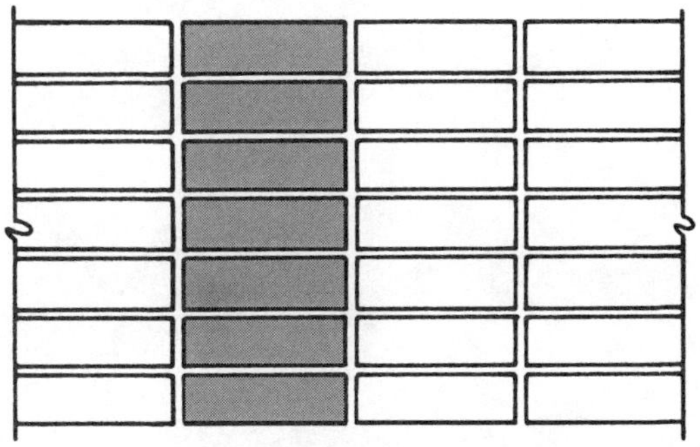

C

D

10. List four reasons why steel framing is gaining acceptance in residential construction. _____

_____

_____

_____

_____

_____

_____

Part V: Problems/Activities

1.

Directions:

Complete the wall framing in each of the problems below by applying the specific requirements.

A. Frame a rough opening that is 52" wide by 40" high. Use a solid (2" × 12") header. Label all framing members and dimension the rough opening and height from the floor to the top of the opening.

B. In these two problems, complete the plan view framing for a corner formed with three full studs (left) and a wall intersecting at a stud (right).

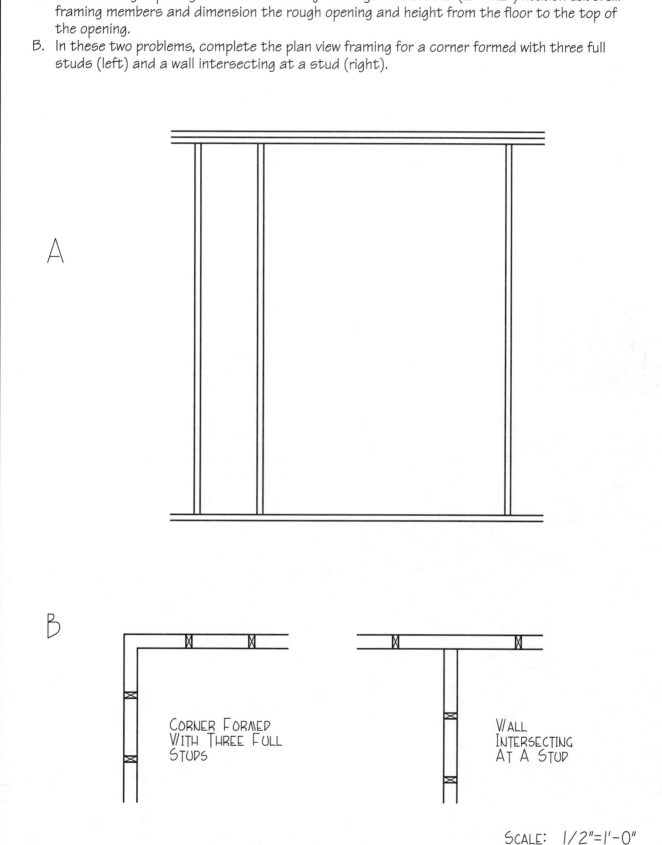

A

B

CORNER FORMED
WITH THREE FULL
STUDS

WALL
INTERSECTING
AT A STUD

SCALE: 1/2"=1'-0"

WALL FRAMING DETAILS	NAME:	14-1

2.

Directions:
Draw a large scale symbol (elevation view at 1/2″ = 1′-0″) for each of the exterior masonry walls indicated below. Refer to the chapter and the reference section in the text. Fill the space provided.

CONCRETE BLOCK

BRICK

ASHLAR STONE

RANDOM RUBBLE STONE

STUCCO

UNCOURSED COBWEB

SCALE: 1/2″=1′-0″

| MASONRY WALL SYMBOLS | NAME: | 14-2 |

15 Doors and Windows

Text, Pages 319–351

Name _____

Course _____ Date _____ Score _____

Part I: Multiple Choice

Select the best answer and write the corresponding letter in the space provided.

1. Which of the following is a type of interior door?

    A. Awning.
    B. Double-action.
    C. Clerestory.
    D. All of the above.

1. _____

2. Metal bi-fold doors are usually _____ thick and commonly used as closet doors.

    A. 1″
    B. 1-1/8″
    C. 1-1/4″
    D. 1-1/2″

2. _____

3. Sliding or bypass doors are:

    A. Used frequently for large openings.
    B. Not subject to warping.
    C. Limited to two doors for each opening.
    D. All of the above.

3. _____

4. Double-action doors are:

    A. Used for large openings.
    B. Hinged to swing through an arc of 180°.
    C. Made of metal and usually 1″ thick.
    D. All of the above.

4. _____

5. Accordion doors:

    A. Require little space.
    B. Are produced in a large variety of materials and designs.
    C. May use individual hinged panels.
    D. All of the above.

5. _____

6. Exterior glass doors are:

    A. Usually hollow cored.
    B. Frequently used between kitchens and dining rooms.
    C. Thicker than interior doors.
    D. None of the above.

6. _____

7. Door jambs used in residential construction are:

    A. Usually made of bronze.
    B. Composed of two side jambs and a head jamb.
    C. 1-3/4″ thick for exterior doors and 1″ thick for interior doors.
    D. All of the above.

7. _____

8. Which of these statements should you follow when planning the windows for a dwelling?

    A. To gain the maximum amount of light possible, place primary windows on the west.
    B. Four small windows will yield less contrast than one large window.
    C. Glass area equal to at least 20% of the floor area should provide adequate natural light.
    D. The best distribution of light is achieved by placing all of the windows on one wall.

8. _____

9. To provide ample ventilation in a home:

    A. The openings for ventilation should be at least 10% of the floor area.
    B. Windows should be placed to receive prevailing breezes.
    C. Plan the location of windows for the best movement of air across a room.
    D. All of the above.

9. _____

10. Windows of the same general type purchased from different manufacturers will seldom have:

    A. Different specifications.
    B. Uniform specifications.
    C. Specifications that are not important to the designer or contractor.
    D. None of the above.

10. _____

11. The rough framed space in the wall needed to install the window is the:

    A. Glass size.
    B. Basic unit.
    C. Rough opening.
    D. Sash opening.

11. _____

12. Casement windows have side-hinged sashes that swing out and may be opened or closed by:

    A. Handles on the sash.
    B. Push-bars on the frame.
    C. Cranks.
    D. All of the above.

12. _____

13. Which of the following lines should be used to show the hinge positions on a hinged window?

    A. Dashed line.
    B. Object line.
    C. Short break line.
    D. Section line.

13. _____

14. Which of the following statements best represents hopper windows?

    A. Hopper windows rarely interfere with the interior space.
    B. Hopper windows are more efficient when placed low on the wall because they direct air upward.
    C. Hopper windows swing outward.
    D. Hopper windows are difficult to operate and maintain.

14. _____

15. Picture windows may:

    A. Be opened to provide ventilation.
    B. Require custom-made screens.
    C. Be large fixed glass units used with other window types.
    D. None of the above.

15. _____

16. The side units in a bay window are normally placed at _____ to the exterior wall.

    A. 90°
    B. 60°
    C. 45°
    D. None of the above.

16. _____

17. Bow window units normally use from _____ casement units to form the arc.

    A. three to six
    B. four to seven
    C. five to eight
    D. Any of the above.

17. _____

18. Which of the following is a characteristic of clerestory windows?

    A. They are placed high on the wall.
    B. They are often installed in the roof of a dwelling.
    C. They are typically fixed windows.
    D. None of the above.

18. _____

Part II: Completion

Complete each sentence with the proper response. Place your answer on the space provided.

1. Interior flush doors are normally covered with 1/8" plywood of mahogany or _____ and are smooth on both sides.

1. _____

2. Pocket doors are a variation of the sliding door and are often used between the _____ and dining room.

2. _____

3. Accordion doors are available in wood, _____, and plastics.

3. _____

4. The top half of a(n) _____ door may operate separately from the bottom half.

4. _____

5. Exterior flush doors are commonly 1-3/4" thick and _____ high.

5. _____

6. Exterior panel doors are produced in white pine, _____ fir, and various other woods.

6. _____

7. To provide for an automatic garage door opener, allow extra headroom above the open door to mount the _____ on the ceiling.

7. _____

8. The information listed in the door schedule is obtained from _____.

8. _____

9. In frame construction, the space between the jamb and rough framing is covered with trim called _____.

9. _____

10. A(n) _____ is placed at the bottom of the door opening between the two side jambs. It drains water away from the door.

10. _____

11. Construction details of windows and doors are normally drawn in _____ through the head jamb, side jamb, and sill.

11. _____

12. Extremely bright areas and dark corners are eliminated by proper design and placement of _____.

12. _____

13. A shallow penetration of light over a broad area can be achieved by using short, _____ windows.

13. _____

14. A thin, deep penetration of light can be achieved by using tall, _____ windows.

14. _____

15. Windows placed high on the wall result in a _____ degree of light penetration into the room.

15. _____

Name _____

16. Areas of large glass will make the room size appear _____.

16. _____

17. Three common materials used in the manufacture of window frames are wood, _____, and plastics.

17. _____

18. Window sashes are held in place by _____ devices or are counterbalanced.

18. _____

19. The overall dimensions of the window unit represent the _____ unit size.

19. _____

20. Narrow, horizontal glass slats are the components of a _____ window.

20. _____

21. _____ windows are circular windows typically installed above another window.

21. _____

22. _____ windows may be custom made in various shapes and sizes from window manufacturers.

22. _____

23. Casement windows are usually placed _____ degrees to the exterior wall in a box bay window.

23. _____

24. Most skylights are _____ in shape to fit between roof trusses; custom-made units are possible to accommodate most any design situation.

24. _____

Part III: Short Answer/Listing
Provide brief answers to the following questions.

1. Which materials are commonly used for the panels of panel doors? _____

_____

2. List one advantage and two disadvantages of pocket doors. _____

_____

_____

3. Where are French doors often used? _____

_____

4. What are the basic differences between interior and exterior doors? _____

_____

_____

5. Name the two most frequently used garage door widths in residential construction. _____

_____

6. Where would a door schedule be found in a set of drawings? _____

_____

7. What is the purpose of a door jamb? _____

_____

8. Why are rough openings framed with extra space in the length and width for interior doors?

_____

_____

_____

9. Which materials are most commonly used in the construction of window and door sills? ___

_____

_____

_____

10. List three factors you should consider when planning the location of a window to take advantage of a pleasing view. _____

_____

_____

11. When selecting windows, first consider the interior requirements. However, what can be done to improve the outside appearance of the home and add to the continuity of the exterior design? _____

_____

_____

12. What is meant by the sash opening? _____

_____

_____

13. When would it be wise to draw a section of the support mullion?_____

_____

14. List four variations of circle top windows commonly used in residential construction. _____

_____

15. List the specific information commonly found on a window schedule._____

_____

_____

_____

Name _____

Part IV: Matching
Match the correct term with its description listed below. Place the corresponding letter on the space provided.

A. Awning.
B. Brick mold.
C. Drip cap.
D. Double-hung.
E. Fixed.
F. Glass size.

G. Glider.
H. Mullions.
I. Muntins.
J. Prehung doors.
K. Rails.
L. Stiles.

1. Vertical members of a panel door.

1. _____

2. Horizontal members of a panel door.

2. _____

3. Units consisting of the jamb and door ready for installation.

3. _____

4. A strip used in frame construction to shed water over a door or window.

4. _____

5. Used in a masonry wall to cover the space between the jamb and the rough framing.

5. _____

6. Windows with two sashes that slide up and down in grooves.

6. _____

7. Small or thin vertical or horizontal bars that divide the glass area into smaller sections.

7. _____

8. Vertical or horizontal components that divide window units.

8. _____

9. Comparable to the inside sash dimensions.

9. _____

10. Also known as horizontal sliding windows.

10. _____

11. Top-hinged windows that swing out at an angle.

11. _____

12. Circle top, picture, and random-shaped windows are examples of this window type.

12. _____

Part V: Problems/Activities

1.

Directions:
Draw a plan view symbol for each of the door types specified below.

FLUSH OR PANEL DOOR   BI-FOLD DOORS

DUTCH DOOR   ACCORDION DOOR

POCKET DOOR   SLIDING (BYPASS) DOORS

DOUBLE-ACTION DOOR   FRENCH DOORS

EXTERIOR PANEL DOOR   SLIDING GLASS DOOR

GARAGE DOOR

SCALE: 1/4"=1'-0"

| PLAN VIEW DOOR SYMBOLS | NAME: | 15-1 |

2.

Directions:
Draw a plan view symbol for each of the window types specified below.

DOUBLE-HUNG WINDOW

AWNING WINDOW

CASEMENT WINDOW (TWO SASH)

FIXED WINDOW

HORIZONTAL SLIDING WINDOW

HOPPER WINDOW

DOUBLE-HUNG 45° BAY WINDOW

FIVE-UNIT CASEMENT BOW WINDOW

SCALE: 1/4"=1'-0"

| PLAN VIEW WINDOW SYMBOLS | NAME: | 15-2 |

3.

Directions:
Label the parts indicated on the exterior door details below.

Head jamb

Head jamb

Side jamb

Side jamb

Sill

Sill

Brick veneer

Frame

Stairs

16

Name _____

Course _____ Date _____ Score _____

Part I: Matching
Match the correct term with its description listed below. Place the corresponding letter on the space provided.

A. Balusters
B. Circular
C. L
D. Landing
E. Newel
F. Nosing
G. Open

H. Plain stringer
I. Rise
J. Riser
K. Run
L. Stairway
M. Stairwell
N. Straight run

O. Stringer
P. Total rise
Q. Total run
R. Tread
S. U
T. Winder

1. A series of steps connecting two or more levels of a structure.

1. _____

2. Stairs that require a long open space.

2. _____

3. A type of stairs with one landing at some point in the middle of the run.

3. _____

4. Stairs with two flights of steps parallel.

4. _____

5. Stairs with pie-shaped steps in place of the middle landing.

5. _____

6. The basic shape of these stairs stems from an irregular curve or arc.

6. _____

7. Vertical components that support the handrail on open stairs.

7. _____

8. Floor area at the top, bottom, or along the flight of stairs.

8. _____

9. The primary posts of the handrail.

9. _____

10. The rounded tread overhang that extends past the face of the riser.

10. _____

11. Stairs without walls on one or both sides.

11. _____

12. A stringer notched or cut to fit the shape of the steps.

12. _____

13. Vertical distance from the surface of one tread to the surface of the next tread.

13. _____

14. Vertical face of a step.

14. _____

15. Distance from the face of one riser to the face of the next riser.

15. _____

16. Opening in which a set of stairs is constructed.

16. _____

17. A structural member that supports the treads and risers.

17. _____

18. The total vertical height of the stairs.

18. _____

19. The total horizontal length of the stairs.

19. _____

20. The horizontal member of each step.

20. _____

Part II: Completion
Complete each sentence with the proper response. Place your answer on the space provided.

1. The prime considerations in stair design should be easy ascent/descent and _____.

1. _____

2. _____ stairs are usually made from construction lumber, constructed on the site, and steeper than main stairs.

2. _____

3. Wide U stairs have a well between the two flights. In _____ U stairs, the space is small or nonexistent.

3. _____

4. In homes where little space is available, _____ stairs may be a solution.

4. _____

5. _____ stairs require a lot of space and are expensive to build.

5. _____

6. A _____ is sometimes called the carriage.

6. _____

7. The main stairway should be at least _____ wide.

7. _____

8. When constructing plain stringers, nail the treads and risers directly to the _____.

8. _____

9. Glue and _____ hold the treads and risers in place permanently on plain stringer stairs.

9. _____

10. On housed stringers, _____ hold the treads and risers in place; all three components are then glued and nailed.

10. _____

Part III: Short Answer/Listing
Provide brief answers to the following questions.

1. What is the term used to describe a set of L stairs that has a landing near the top or bottom?

_____

2. In a set of winder stairs, how is the width of the "pie-shaped" steps determined? _____

_____

_____

Name _____

3. List the three factors to consider when designing a set of stairs._____

_____

_____

4. In a set of stairs requiring more than two stringers, where should the third stringer be placed?

_____

5. List advantages and disadvantages of plain stringer stair construction. _____

_____

_____

6. What method is commonly used to hold the treads and risers in housed stairs?_____

_____

_____

7. What is the ideal range for riser height? _____

_____

8. List the four rules to follow when determining the rise-run ratio. _____

Rule 1: _____

Rule 2: _____

Rule 3: _____

Rule 4: _____

9. Why is there always one less tread than there are risers?_____

_____

10. Label the drawings of the general types of stairs below.

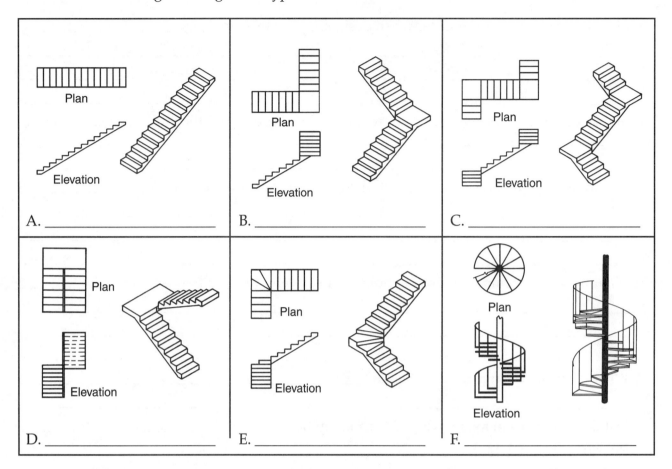

A. _____

B. _____

C. _____

D. _____

E. _____

F. _____

11. Locate and label the items identified on the stairway drawing below.

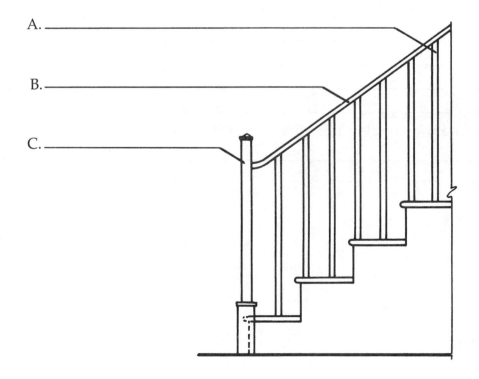

A. _____

B. _____

C. _____

12. Calculate the following design elements for a set of stairs for a two-story home. The total rise is 72", with a standard tread of 11-1/2". A 1" nosing is required and the stairs should have an acceptable slope of 30° to 35°. Calculate the following:

Total Run = _____

Number of Risers = _____

Riser Height = _____

Number of Treads = _____

Run of a Step = _____

Part IV: Multiple Choice

Select the best answer and write the corresponding letter in the space provided.

1. Of the following house styles, which is most likely to have stairs?

    A. Garrison.
    B. Salt box.
    C. Southern colonial.
    D. All of the above.

1. _____

2. The type of stairs used most in residential construction is:

    A. L stairs.
    B. Straight run.
    C. Spiral.
    D. Winder.

2. _____

3. Circular stairs have _____ steps.

    A. triangular
    B. pie-shaped
    C. trapezoidal
    D. winder

3. _____

4. Enclosed stairs are also known as:

    A. Closed stairs.
    B. Housed stairs.
    C. Box stairs.
    D. All of the above.

4. _____

5. Plain stringers are constructed for:

    A. Uncarpeted main stairs.
    B. Service stairs.
    C. Circular stairs.
    D. All of the above.

5. _____

6. Housed stringers are:

    A. Constructed from finished lumber.
    B. Usually purchased precut or preassembled.
    C. Sometimes made from 1" × 12" or 2" × 12" lumber.
    D. All of the above.

7. The actual size of an oak tread used in housed stringer construction is _____ thick.

    A. 3/4"
    B. 1"
    C. 1-1/16"
    D. 1-1/4"

8. All stairs should have at least one handrail. The recommended handrail/guardrail height is:

    A. 30" along the incline and 36" at the landing.
    B. 32" along the incline and 36" at the landing.
    C. 34" along the incline and 38" at the landing.
    D. None of the above.

9. Minimum stairway headroom is:

    A. 6'-0"
    B. 6'-6"
    C. 7'-0"
    D. 7'-5"

10. Recent code changes require handrails for:

    A. All stairs, but not ramps.
    B. Steep stairs.
    C. All stairs and ramps.
    D. Handrails were not addressed.

6. _____

7. _____

8. _____

9. _____

10. _____

Part V: Problems/Activities

1.

Directions:

Problem A—Draw the plan view and elevation in section of plain stringer stairs that meet the following specifications: width = 36", tread width = 11-1/2", riser height = 7-1/4", nosing = 1", stringer is 2" × 12", number of risers is 6, and the total run is 52.5".

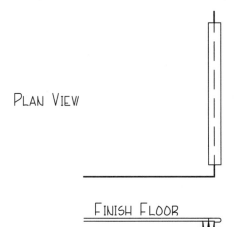

PLAN VIEW

SCALE: 1/2"=1'-0"

FINISH FLOOR

ELEVATION SECTION

FINISH FLOOR

Problem B—Draw a detail (scale: 1" = 1'-0") of housed stringer stairs showing 5/4" oak treads, 1" pine risers, 2" × 12" vertical grain fir stringers, and wedges. Label and show dimensions.

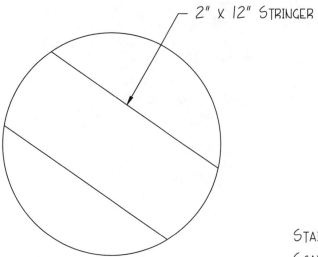

2" × 12" STRINGER

STAIR DETAIL
SCALE: 1"=1'-0"

STAIRS	NAME:	16-1

2. **Stair Details.** This assignment will be evaluated based on the following factors: Quality of work, design parameters met, accurately and completely communicated design, and directions followed.

Directions. Your task is to design a set of enclosed straight run main stairs. Show both a plan view and elevation in section. The stairs are between the first and second floors of a residence. The scale is to be 1"=1'-0". Include these elements in your design:

- Finished-floor-to-finished-floor distance (total rise) is 9'-1/2" (2" × 12" joists, 1/2" drywall, and 3/4" finished floor).

- Minimum headroom is 6'-6".

- Width of stairs (outside to outside of stringers) is 36".

- Stairs use housed stringer with wedges and glue.

- Treads are 5/4" oak, risers are white pine, and stringers are 2" × 12" oak.

- Use standard 11-1/2" wide treads and allow a 1" nosing.

- Angle of the stairs must be between 30° and 37°.

- Indicate stairwell dimensions with a minimum headroom of 6'-6".

- Show handrail of your design on the elevation section drawing.

- Show all dimensions and necessary notes.

- Prepare a stair data chart that shows:
  Total rise
  Total run
  Rise of a step
  Run of a step
  Width of the stair
  Angle of stairs
  Stairwell opening
  Nosing
  Handrail height

- Be sure the views project. Include all material symbols, scale, and title block.

Fireplaces, Chimneys, and Stoves

17

Text, Pages 369–387

Name _____

Course _____ Date _____ Score _____

Part I: Completion
Complete each sentence with the proper response. Place your answer on the space provided.

1. Fireplaces may either be gas-fired or _____ burning.

   1. _____

2. The hearth should be made from _____ materials such as ceramic tile, stone, or slate.

   2. _____

3. If the fireplace is giving off only a small amount of heat, then the fire chamber is probably too _____.

   3. _____

4. A fireplace that smokes into the room is likely to be the result of a fire chamber that is too _____.

   4. _____

5. Ashes are removed from the ash chamber through the _____.

   5. _____

6. The _____ and _____ of a prefabricated steel heat-circulating fireplace are made with a double-wall passageway where the air is heated.

   6. _____

7. The _____ opens to the back of the fireplace throat.

   7. _____

8. The smoke shelf height is determined by the location of the _____.

   8. _____

9. The flue starts at the top of the smoke chamber and proceeds to the top of the _____.

   9. _____

10. Each fireplace in a structure must have its own _____.

    10. _____

11. _____ is reduced when the flue is not straight.

    11. _____

12. A rule of thumb to follow in selecting the proper flue size is that the cross-sectional area of the flue should be at least _____ of the fireplace opening.

    12. _____

13. A warmer chimney results in _____ performance.

    13. _____

14. The chimney does not support any part of the house; thus it is a _____ structure.

    14. _____

15. The recommended clearance for framing members around a chimney is _____.

    15. _____

16. The space between the chimney and the framing should be filled with a _____ material.

16. _____

17. The chance of water problems is _____ if a chimney is placed at the peak or ridge line of a roof.

17. _____

18. Wide chimneys or extremely low roof slopes usually require a _____ along the chimney.

18. _____

19. _____ are the most popular type and the least complicated to construct of all the fireplace types.

19. _____

20. The three-face fireplace is also referred to as a _____ fireplace.

20. _____

21. The _____ type of stove provides more even heat.

21. _____

22. Medium efficiency stoves have less air leakage into the stove, have better combustion, and are _____ to 50% efficient.

22. _____

Part II: Multiple Choice
Select the best answer and write the corresponding letter in the space provided.

1. The hearth should extend _____ in front of the fireplace.

1. _____

   A. 12"
   B. 14"
   C. 16"
   D. 18"

2. The walls of the fire chamber should be a minimum of _____ thick.

2. _____

   A. 8"
   B. 9"
   C. 10"
   D. 12"

3. Prefabricated steel heat-circulating fireplaces are:

3. _____

   A. Somewhat efficient.
   B. Very efficient.
   C. Inefficient.
   D. None of the above.

4. Fireplace dampers:

4. _____

   A. Prevent downdrafts of cold air when the fireplace is not being used.
   B. Are made of cast iron or steel.
   C. Should be located 6" or 8" above the top of the fireplace opening.
   D. All of the above.

5. The shape of the smoke chamber is:

    A. Basically square.
    B. An elongated rectangle.
    C. Basically a pyramid with the back side usually vertical.
    D. None of the above.

5. _____

6. The flue lining is usually made from:

    A. Clay.
    B. Concrete block.
    C. Firebrick.
    D. Poured concrete.

6. _____

7. There should be _____ of masonry placed on all sides of the flue with a lining.

    A. 6″
    B. 5″
    C. 4″
    D. 3″

7. _____

8. At least _____ of masonry should be placed on all sides of the flue when it does not have a lining.

    A. 8″
    B. 6″
    C. 4″
    D. 2″

8. _____

9. Assume that you have designed a fireplace for a new home. The opening measures 48″ wide by 32″ high. What size modular flue is recommended for this size fireplace? Refer to the Design Data for Single-Face Fireplaces chart shown in Figure 17-15 in the text.

    A. 12″ × 16″
    B. 16″ × 16″
    C. 16″ × 20″
    D. 20″ × 20″

9. _____

10. Most building codes require that a flue be at least _____ above the highest point of the roof to prevent sparks flying out of the flue and setting the roof on fire.

    A. 2′
    B. 3′
    C. 4′
    D. 5′

10. _____

11. Most lintels used to support the masonry above fire-place openings are:

    A. Wood beams.
    B. Cast concrete.
    C. Lintel blocks.
    D. Angle steel.

11. _____

12. The two-face adjacent fireplace:

    A. Usually functions more efficiently than other fire-place types.
    B. Opens on the front and either left or right side.
    C. Is not subject to drafts.
    D. All of the above.

12. _____

13. Prefabricated steel heat-circulating fireplaces may require:

    A. Framing enclosures.
    B. Masonry enclosures.
    C. Fruitwood logs.
    D. A and B.

13. _____

14. High-efficiency stoves, which are over 50% efficient, use _____ to increase output.

    A. chimneys
    B. bellows
    C. heat exchange devices
    D. All of the above.

14. _____

Part III: Short Answer/Listing

Provide brief answers to the following questions.

1. Name the five different types of fireplaces. _____

_____

_____

2. Which material is normally used for the inner hearth? _____

3. What is the purpose of fireclay and where might it be used? _____

_____

4. Why is the design of the fire chamber important? _____

_____

_____

5. Explain how a prefabricated steel, heat-circulating fireplace gains additional efficiency. _____

_____

_____

_____

6. What is the function of the smoke shelf? _____

_____

Name _____

7. Which materials are commonly used in the construction of the smoke chamber? _____
   _____

8. What is the rule of thumb to follow when selecting a flue for a fireplace opening? _____
   _____

9. List two circumstances that would require increasing the size of the flue. _____
   _____
   _____

10. How many flues may a single chimney have? _____

11. List four appliances or features of a home that require their own flue. _____
    _____

12. List two framing members used to provide support in the opening through which a chimney
    passes. _____

13. When chimneys are placed along a single slope of the roof, water can back up and seep under
    the shingles and produce leaks. What steps can be taken to prevent this? _____
    _____
    _____
    _____

14. Why would a fireplace insert be used? _____
    _____
    _____

15. List the two combustion materials (solids) used by stoves. _____
    _____

16. How do radiant stoves and circulating stoves differ? _____
    _____
    _____
    _____

17. Which of the two types of stoves—radiant or circulating—has a lower surface temperature?
    _____

18. List three examples of low-efficiency stoves. _____
    _____

19. When installing a stove in front of a fireplace opening, what should be done to reflect the heat
    back into the room? _____
    _____

20. What effect will extending the height of a chimney have on the draft? _____
    _____

Part IV: Matching

Match the correct term with its description listed below. Place the corresponding letter on the space provided.

A. Ash chamber
B. Damper
C. Ash dump
D. Fireclay
E. Flue
F. Hearth
G. Lintel
H. Saddle

I. Single-face
J. Smoke chamber
K. Smoke shelf
L. Stove
M. Three-face
N. Two-face (adjacent)
O. Two-face (opposite)

1. Protects the floor from sparks.

1. _____

2. Fire-resistant mortar.

2. _____

3. Opening in the fireplace floor with a metal trap door.

3. _____

4. Holds ashes after they are removed from the fire chamber.

4. _____

5. Regulates the flow of air.

5. _____

6. Prevents down rushing cold air from forcing smoke into the room.

6. _____

7. The space directly above the smoke shelf and damper.

7. _____

8. Supplies a smoke path from the fireplace.

8. _____

9. Designed to shed water away from the chimney.

9. _____

10. Supports the masonry above a fireplace opening.

10. _____

11. Most popular type of fireplace.

11. _____

12. A fireplace that is open on both front and back sides.

12. _____

13. Also known as a projecting corner fireplace.

13. _____

14. A fireplace that is open on three sides.

14. _____

15. A good choice for localized heat source.

15. _____

Part V: Problems/Activities

1.

Directions:
Study the pictorial section of a fireplace and chimney below and identify each of the materials, parts, etc., indicated by the leaders. Use these specific notes:

- > Ash pit
- > Ash dump
- > Cleanout door
- > Damper
- > Double header
- > Face brick
- > Firebrick
- > Floor joist

- > Smoke chamber
- > Smoke shelf
- > Steel lintel
- > Stone hearth
- > 4" Reinforced concrete inner hearth
- > Minimum thickness of walls of fire chamber is 8"
- > Flue lining

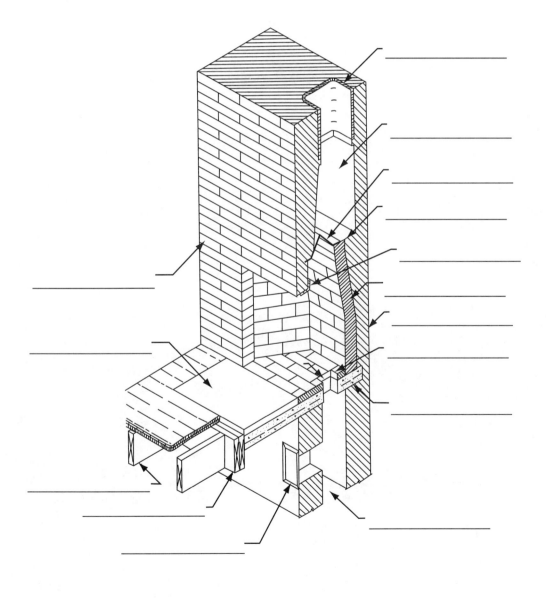

FIREPLACE PARTS	NAME:	17-1

2.

Directions:
Using the Design Data for Single Face Fireplaces chart in Figure 17-15 in the text, fill in the dimensions represented on the drawings for a 40″ wide fireplace and modular flue liner. Do not scale the drawings to arrive at these dimensions.

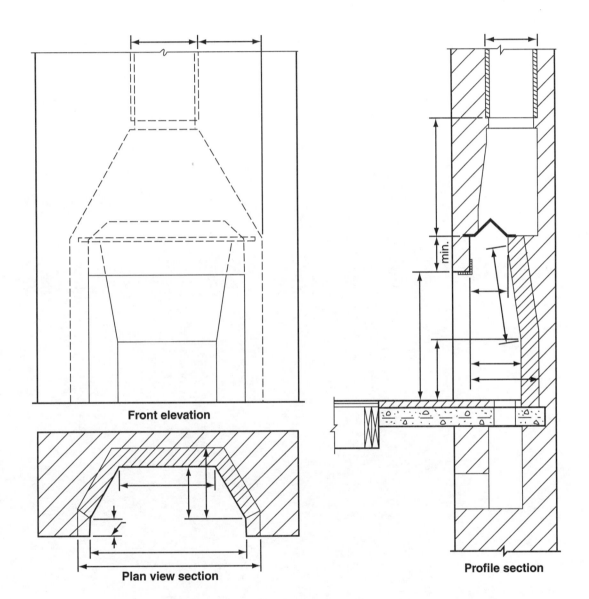

Front elevation

Plan view section

Profile section

3. **Fireplace Details.** This assignment will be evaluated based on the following factors: Quality of work, design parameters met, accurately and completely communicated design, and directions followed.

Directions. You are to design a single-face masonry fireplace. Show the design using a plan view in section, front elevation, and profile section from the footing to the top of the chimney. The scale is to be 1/2″ = 1′-0″. Use a sheet of C-size paper. Include the following elements in your design.

- The fireplace is for a ranch-style house that has a 24″ crawl space. A 12″ × 12″ ash cleanout is located in the crawl space.
- The masonry chimney is 28″ × 60″ × the necessary height. The facing is brick and the chimney structure is concrete block.
- The fireplace opening is 36″ wide with an 18″ × 60″ sandstone outer hearth.
- A 2″ × 3″ angle steel support should be used above the fireplace opening for the brick ledge. The flue damper is cast iron; see the text for dimensions.
- The inner and outer hearth should be supported on a 4″ reinforced concrete slab.
- The fire pit should be lined on all sides with firebrick (2-1/2″ × 5″ × 9″) and provide a 5″ × 9″ ash dump.
- Use 12″ modular clay flue tile.
- Plan the height of the chimney for a structure with a 5:12 pitch roof and a total rise of 6′-0″ at the peak. The chimney passes through the ridge.
- The top of the chimney is between 2′ and 3′ above the highest point of the roof and has a 4″ concrete cap. Show roof flashing where appropriate.
- All dimensions should conform to design data presented in the text.
- Views should project.

The Floor Plan

18

Text, Pages 389–408

Name _____

Course _____ Date _____ Score _____

Part I: Short Answer/Listing
Provide brief answers to the following questions.

1. List nine features that are generally shown on the floor plan. _____

_____

_____

_____

_____

_____

_____

2. What stairway information should be included on the floor plan?_____

_____

_____

_____

3. What fireplace/chimney information should be included on the floor plan? _____

_____

_____

_____

4. Is it necessary to indicate the size of the various rooms on the floor plan? If so, where should the information be included? _____

_____

5. Dimension lines should be placed away from the view to prevent crowding. How far out should they be placed? _____

6. Where should the scale be located on the drawing? _____

7. Where should the number of each sheet be placed? _____

_____

8. Before starting the steps to draw the floor plan, what preliminary work should be done?

_____

_____

9. What is the first step in drawing a floor plan? _____
_____

10. If the house will have stairs, what preliminary work should be done before the stairs can be drawn? _____
_____
_____

11. When should dimensions, notes, and room names be added to the floor plan?_____
_____

12. What information should be included in the title block? _____
_____
_____
_____

13. Why are expansion plans advisable? _____
_____
_____

14. Exterior frame walls are dimensioned to the outside of the stud wall. From the stud, what does the "outside" usually include? _____

15. What is the actual thickness of an exterior stud wall composed of the following materials: 1/2″ drywall, 2″ × 4″ studs, 3/4″ rigid foam insulation, and 1/2″ plywood siding? _____

16. In CADD, windows and doors can be inserted from a _____ library.

Part II: Multiple Choice

Select the best answer and write the corresponding letter in the space provided.

1. Work on the floor plan is normally started: 1. _____

   A. First.
   B. Last.
   C. After the elevations.
   D. After the electrical plan.

2. The floor plan is actually a(n):   2. _____

   A. Top view.
   B. Elevation view.
   C. Section view.
   D. None of the above.

3. In manual drafting, interior stud walls with drywall on   3. _____
   both sides may be drawn as a _____ nominal thickness;
   however, in CADD, the actual dimension should be
   used.

   A. 4″ or 8″
   B. 5″
   C. 6″
   D. 8″, 10″, or 12″

4. The _____ opening should be shown for windows.

    A. rough
    B. sash width
    C. finished
    D. None of the above.

4. _____

5. The _____ door width should be used for doors.

    A. actual
    B. rough
    C. finished
    D. None of the above.

5. _____

6. Which linetype (symbol) is used to show an archway or plain opening on a floor plan?

    A. Object line.
    B. Cutting-plane line.
    C. Hidden line.
    D. Centerline.

6. _____

7. Information on patios and swimming pools that is included on the floor plan may be:

    A. Location.
    B. Size.
    C. Materials.
    D. All of the above.

7. _____

8. The name of the room should be placed near the center of the room. It should be lettered _____ high to draw attention to it.

    A. 1/16″
    B. 1/8″
    C. 3/16″
    D. 1/4″

8. _____

9. In architectural drawing, dimension lines are continuous lines with the figure placed:

    A. At the end of the line.
    B. Above the line.
    C. Under the line.
    D. At the beginning of the line.

9. _____

10. Recommended spacing between dimension lines is:

    A. 1/4″ or 3/8″
    B. 3/8″ or 1/2″
    C. 1/2″ or 5/8″
    D. None of the above.

10. _____

11. Which of the following methods of showing a dimension is proper?

   A. 18″
   B. 1′-6″
   C. Both A and B.
   D. None of the above.

11. _____

12. The preferred method of dimensioning interior walls is to the:

   A. Inside of the wall.
   B. Outside of the wall.
   C. Center.
   D. All of the above.

12. _____

13. Overall width and length of major wall segments should be multiples of _____ to comply with building material sizes.

   A. 4′
   B. 6′
   C. 8′
   D. 10′

13. _____

14. The scale commonly used for residential floor plans is:

   A. Half size
   B. 1″ = 1′-0″
   C. 1/2″ = 1′-0″
   D. 1/4″ = 1′-0″

14. _____

15. After the exterior walls have been completed, draw the:

   A. Windows and doors.
   B. Interior walls.
   C. Stairs.
   D. Title block and scale.

15. _____

16. In manual drafting, the interior and exterior wall construction lines may be darkened after:

   A. The doors, windows, stairs, and fireplaces have been drawn.
   B. The kitchen cabinets, appliances, and bathroom fixtures are drawn.
   C. Checking the drawing for accuracy.
   D. Construction is underway.

16. _____

17. Outside features such as patios, walks, or decks should be drawn:

   A. Before the exterior walls are drawn.
   B. After the house has been built.
   C. Before the kitchen cabinets, appliances, and bathroom fixtures have been drawn.
   D. After all interior features have been drawn.

17. _____

Name _____

18. Base cabinets for kitchens are drawn _____ deep while wall cabinets are _____ deep.

    A. 24"; 12"
    B. 12"; 24"
    C. 16"; 10"
    D. 36"; 24"

18. _____

19. The material symbols should be added:

    A. When the design elements that use these materials are drawn.
    B. Only if the contractor wants them drawn.
    C. At any time.
    D. When the drawing is almost complete.

19. _____

20. Object lines, hidden lines, centerlines, etc., should:

    A. Be the same width.
    B. Be erased.
    C. Vary in width.
    D. None of the above.

20. _____

21. Which of the following is *not* an advantage of CADD over manual drafting?

    A. Automatic wall generation.
    B. Elimination of hand lettering.
    C. Style of drawing.
    D. Repetitive use of symbols.

21. _____

Part III: Matching

Match the correct term or symbol with its description listed below. Place the corresponding letter on the blank at right.

A. Dimensions
B. Floor plan
C. Hidden line

D.

E.

F.

G.

H.

I.

J.

K.

L.

M.

1. The heart of a set of construction drawings.

2. Frame wall.

3. Concrete block wall.

4. Solid brick wall.

5. Brick veneer and frame wall.

6. Linetype (symbol) used to indicate an archway.

7. Flashing.

8. Rigid insulation.

9. Batt insulation.

10. Cast concrete.

11. Finished board.

12. Dimensional lumber.

13. Shows the size of a feature or its location on a floor plan.

1. _____

2. _____

3. _____

4. _____

5. _____

6. _____

7. _____

8. _____

9. _____

10. _____

11. _____

12. _____

13. _____

Part IV: Completion

Complete each sentence with the proper response. Place your answer on the space provided.

1. For a less complex structure, the floor plan may be combined with the electrical plan, heating/cooling plan, or _____ plan.

1. _____

2. Brick exterior walls are generally _____ nominal thickness.

2. _____

Name _____

3. When drawing a floor plan using CADD, use the _____, _____, or similar command to draw the wall at the proper thickness.

4. A _____ should be drawn through the middle of the opening for windows in frame walls.

5. Sills are drawn for _____ and _____.

6. The _____ indicates which way the door will open.

7. _____ should be used on drawings to indicate construction materials.

8. Dimensions should always be oriented _____ to the dimension line.

9. Leaders should be a maximum of _____ in length.

10. Dimension solid masonry walls to the _____ of the wall.

11. Dimension brick veneer walls to the _____ of the _____ wall.

12. Include the overall dimensions for the length and _____ of the building.

13. Either a(n) _____ or _____ symbol may be used to identify the fireplace.

14. The size and _____ of fireplace must be indicated on the floor plan.

15. Wall cabinets should be drawn with a(n) _____ linetype.

16. It is important to show dimensions for all _____ wall features on the wall where they are located.

17. Guidelines should be left on the drawing, but _____ lines may be removed.

18. After the drawing is complete, examine the entire drawing for _____ and completeness.

19. Openings in a concrete or masonry wall are generally dimensioned to the _____ of the opening.

20. In a frame wall, a door or window is dimensioned to _____ of the rough opening.

3. _____

_____

4. _____

5. _____

_____

6. _____

7. _____

8. _____

9. _____

10. _____

11. _____

_____

12. _____

13. _____

_____

14. _____

15. _____

16. _____

17. _____

18. _____

19. _____

20. _____

Part V: Problems/Activities

1.

Directions:
Complete the plan view of the following symbols that are used on typical residential floor plans.

18-1

Brick Veneer on Frame

Solid Brick Wall

Concrete Block Wall

Case Concrete Wall

Archway or Plain Opening

Glazed Tile
Section

Terrazzo
Section

Slate
Section

Rubble Stone
Section

Scale: 1/4"=1'-0"

| FLOOR PLAN SYMBOLS | NAME: | 18-1 |

2.

Directions:
Using the procedure discussed in the text, properly dimension the frame wall structure and the concrete wall structure examples. Note: The scale is 1/4″ = 1′-0″.

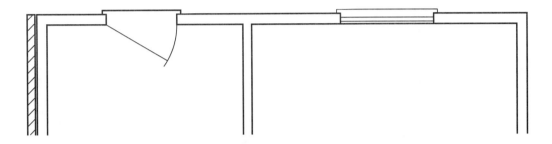

FRAME WALL CONSTRUCTION

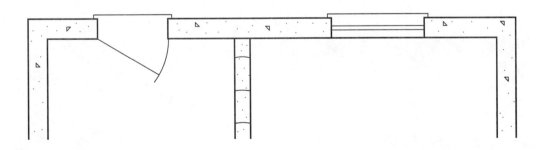

CONCRETE WALL CONSTRUCTION

| DIMENSIONING FLOOR PLANS | NAME: | 18-2 |

3. **Floor Plan.** This assignment will be evaluated based on the following factors: Quality of work, use of proper symbols, proper size of symbols, proper size of features, good planning, proper dimensions, and overall communication provided.

Directions: Study chapters 14, 15, and 18. You are to draw a floor plan for a ranch style house without a basement. Follow the procedure for drawing a floor plan described in the text. Scale is 1/4″ = 1′-0″. Use C-size paper. The design should meet the following criteria:

- Outside dimensions of the house are to be 34′-0″ × 64′-0″. The house may deviate some from these dimensions to accommodate room layout, a porch, and a garage.

- The house should contain a living room, dining area, three bedrooms, kitchen, family room, two baths, and single-car garage.

- Include ample closet space with shelves and rods.

- Exterior doors should be 3′-0″ wide. Interior doors should be 2′-10″ except for baths, which should be 2′-6″ or 2′-8″. Closets may vary depending on the type of door used or closet design.

- Use standard-size appliances, fixtures, and windows.

- Label rooms and show approximate room sizes below the name.

- Completely dimension the floor plan using the procedures described in the text.

- Identify every window and door with a letter or number so that a window and door schedule may be developed.

- Your house may use any standard exterior material that you wish. Interior walls should be framed as 2″ × 4″ studs with 1/2″ drywall on both sides. Wet walls (plumbing walls) may have 2″ × 6″ studs if desired.

- The garage floor should be at least 4″ lower than the house floor.

Roof Designs
19

Name _____

Course _____ Date _____ Score _____

Part I: Multiple Choice
Select the best answer and write the corresponding letter in the space provided.

1. Which of the following characteristics is typical of a gable roof?

   A. Easy to build.
   B. Sheds water well.
   C. Provides for ventilation.
   D. All of the above.

   1. _____

2. A roof type more suited to houses in warm, dry climates than in cold, wet climates is a(n) _____ roof.

   A. flat
   B. hip
   C. shed
   D. A-frame

   2. _____

3. Which of the following is a feature of common rafters?

   A. They run parallel to the top wall plate.
   B. They run parallel to the ridge of the roof.
   C. They extend from the ridge of the roof to the plate or beyond.
   D. None of the above.

   3. _____

4. Which of the following is a roofing material that is light in weight?

   A. Slate
   B. Asphalt shingles
   C. Clay tile
   D. All of the above.

   4. _____

5. The width of a narrow box cornice is normally between:

   A. 4″ and 8″
   B. 5″ and 10″
   C. 6″ and 12″
   D. 7″ and 14″

   5. _____

6. In a(n) _____ cornice, the rafter does not project beyond the wall.

    A. close
    B. open
    C. narrow box
    D. wide box without lookouts

6. _____

7. Which of the following is a feature of lightweight wood roof trusses?

    A. Most lightweight roof trusses can span distances of 50′ to 60′.
    B. Generally, 2″ × 4″ lumber is used in lightweight wood roof trusses.
    C. In most instances, lightweight wood roof trusses are more expensive than traditional roof frame construction.
    D. None of the above.

7. _____

8. The recommended total area of ventilator openings in the attic space should be a minimum of 1/300th of the ceiling area. How much ventilator area should be planned for a house with a ceiling area of 1800 square feet?

    A. At least 6 square feet.
    B. At least 9 square feet.
    C. At least 3 square feet.
    D. None of the above.

8. _____

9. Flashing should be used _____.

    A. where any feature pierces the roof
    B. where a roof attaches to a second-floor wall
    C. next to the chimney
    D. All of the above.

9. _____

10. You can use 6″ or 8″ individual boards as sheathing. For rafters spaced 16″ or 24″OC, the boards should be at least _____ thick.

    A. 1/4″
    B. 1/2″
    C. 3/4″
    D. 1″

10. _____

11. Two requirements of roofing materials are to waterproof the roof and provide many years of service. The most popular type is:

    A. Asphalt
    B. Wood
    C. Clay
    D. None of the above.

11. _____

Name _____

12. When the roof pitch is 12:12 and the span is 24', how high is the roof ridge above the top plate?

    A. 4'
    B. 8'
    C. 12'
    D. 24'

12. _____

Part II: Matching
Match the correct term with its description listed below. Place the corresponding letter on the space provided.

A. A-frame
B. Clear span
C. Cornice
D. Flashing
E. Flat
F. Gable
G. Gusset
H. Hip

I. Mansard
J. Pitch
K. Rake
L. Rise
M. Run
N. Sheathing
O. Shed

1. A type of roof that is easy to build and very popular.

1. _____

2. A popular roof style with a sloped roof section rather than gables at the ends.

2. _____

3. A "built-up" or membrane roof covering is needed for this type of roof.

3. _____

4. This type of roof is similar to a flat roof, but has more pitch.

4. _____

5. A roof type with a French design.

5. _____

6. This roof type forms both the walls plus the roof.

6. _____

7. Also referred to as slope.

7. _____

8. Horizontal distance from the inside of one stud wall to the inside of the opposite stud wall.

8. _____

9. The vertical distance from the top of the wall plate to the underside of the rafters at the ridge.

9. _____

10. Half of the clear span.

10. _____

11. Roof overhang at the eaves line that links the sidewalls and roof.

11. _____

12. Also known as the gable end.

12. _____

13. Wood or metal fastener used in trusses.

13. _____

14. Galvanized sheet metal, aluminum, or copper applied to a roof to prevent water from entering.

14. _____

15. Supports the roofing material.

15. _____

Part III: Short Answer/Listing

Provide brief answers to the following questions.

1. How is a built-up roof made? _____

_____

_____

2. Rafters are cut to the desired measurements by finding four cuts. Name the four cuts.

_____

_____

3. Rafter size is determined by three factors. Name the three factors. _____

_____

_____

4. When would rafters become ceiling joists? _____

_____

_____

5. List three designs where the open cornice may be used. _____

_____

_____

6. When is a wide box cornice without lookouts typically used? _____

_____

_____

7. Where is the soffit material nailed in the wide box cornice without lookouts? _____

_____

_____

8. Wide overhangs are more expensive to build than a close rake; however, wide overhangs do produce two advantages. Name the two advantages. _____

_____

_____

9. The house style often dictates the type of roof or cornice required. What type of cornice is best suited for a colonial or Cape Cod? _____

_____

10. Before ordering wood trusses for a specific structure, what four factors should be known?

_____

_____

11. In some buildings, the bottom chord of the roof trusses extends past the exterior wall. List the advantages that result from this feature. _____

_____

_____

Name _____

12. What are two common ways to ventilate the attic space? _____

_____

_____

13. Other than plywood, list three materials that are commonly used for roof sheathing. _____

_____

_____

14. Name two newer types of roofing materials that have greater wind resistance than traditional asphalt shingles. _____

_____

_____

Part IV: Completion

Complete each sentence with the proper response. Place your answer on the space provided.

1. The least expensive type of roof to construct is the _____ roof.

   1. _____

2. The shed roof may require a built-up roof unless the pitch of the roof is over _____.

   2. _____

3. The _____ roof type is used a great deal on barns.

   3. _____

4. It is good practice to use one of the standard roof _____ or slopes when designing a roof.

   4. _____

5. Light roofing material weighs less than _____ pounds per square foot.

   5. _____

6. The cornice forms on two sides of a _____ roof.

   6. _____

7. In _____ cornices, rafter ends are exposed and generally tapered or curved to eliminate bulk.

   7. _____

8. The soffit board is nailed to the underside of the rafter in a _____ box cornice.

   8. _____

9. Wide box cornices without lookouts have _____ soffits.

   9. _____

10. The span of a gable roof past the end wall of the dwelling is the _____, or gable end.

    10. _____

11. The W-type truss, the _____ truss, and the scissors truss are generally used in residential construction.

    11. _____

12. Two results of a well-ventilated attic are less _____ buildup to cause damage to the underside of the sheathing and a cooler house in the summer.

    12. _____

13. The width of the valley flashing is dependent upon the slope of the roof. A roof slope of 5:12 requires flashing at least _____ wide.

    13. _____

14. Gutters are commonly made from galvanized sheet metal, aluminum, copper, and vinyl. One popular style of aluminum or vinyl gutter is the _____.

14. _____

15. Plywood sheathing should be placed with the _____ perpendicular to the rafters.

15. _____

16. A moisture barrier is required between the sheathing and the shingles. Generally, building paper of 15-pound, saturated _____ provides this barrier.

16. _____

17. _____ is required where any feature, such as a chimney or section of a wall, pierces the roof.

17. _____

18. The area of the roof that includes the overhang forming a connection between the roof and side walls is called the _____.

18. _____

1.

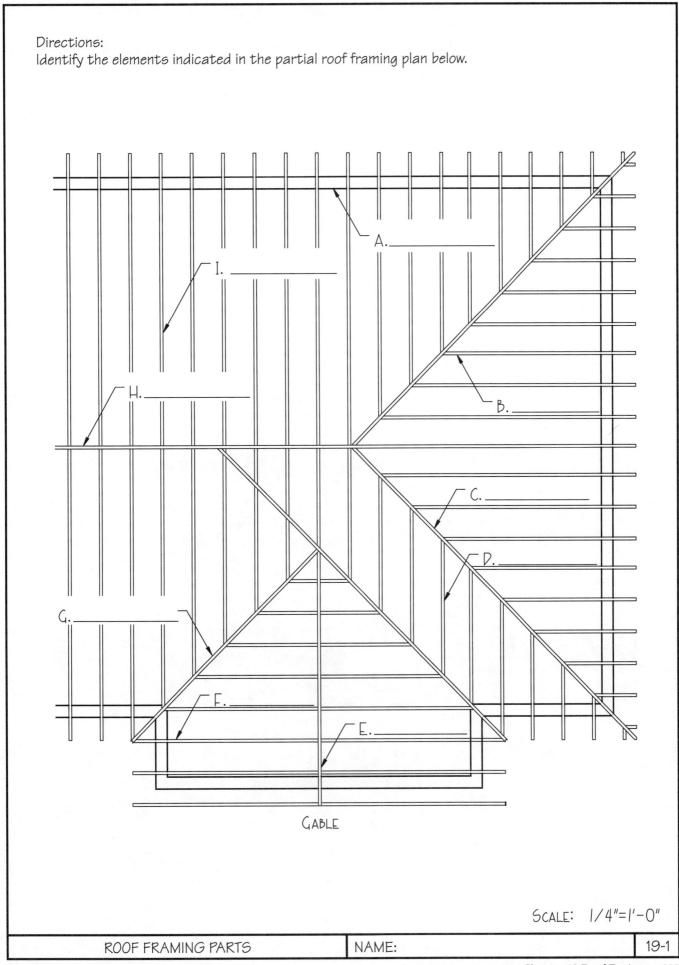

Directions:
Identify the elements indicated in the partial roof framing plan below.

A. _____

I. _____

B. _____

H. _____

C. _____

D. _____

G. _____

F. _____

E. _____

GABLE

SCALE: 1/4"=1'-0"

| ROOF FRAMING PARTS | NAME: | 19-1 |

2.

Directions:

A. Construct the ceiling joist (2″ × 6″) and rafter (2″ × 4″) layout for a cottage that has a clear span of 19′–3 1/2″, a roof slope of 6:12, and an 18″ overhang. Dimension the rise and run and show the roof slope triangle.

B. Instead of ceiling joists and rafters, show the roof structure using W-type or King-post roof trusses. Dimension as above.

A

19′-3 1/2″
CLEAR SPAN

B

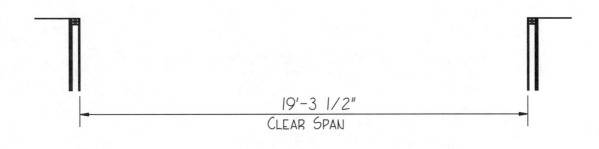

19′-3 1/2″
CLEAR SPAN

SCALE: 1/4″=1′-0″

| ROOF SLOPE | NAME: | 19-2 |

3.

Directions:
Draw a large scale (1″ = 1′-0″) section through a wide box cornice with lookouts. Incorporate the following dimensions and features in your drawing:
> 2″ × 4″ stud wall with 3/4″ RF insulation and horizontal siding on the outside and 1/2″ drywall inside.
> 24″ overhang (outside of insulation to end of rafters) with ventilation.
> 2″ × 6″ rafters and 2″ × 8″ ceiling joists.
> 1/2″ plywood roof sheathing, redwood fascia board, and asphalt shingles.

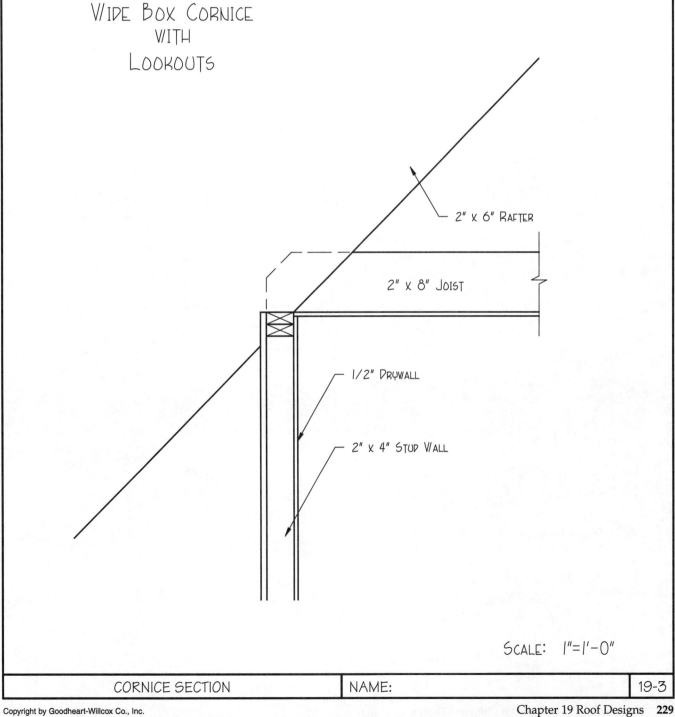

WIDE BOX CORNICE
WITH
LOOKOUTS

2″ × 6″ RAFTER

2″ × 8″ JOIST

1/2″ DRYWALL

2″ × 4″ STUD WALL

SCALE: 1″=1′-0″

| CORNICE SECTION | NAME: | 19-3 |

4.

Factors to be considered in the evaluation of this assignment include quality of your work, application of appropriate construction techniques, use of appropriate size building materials for spans and economy, and overall communication.

Directions:
Study Chapter 19 in the text before attempting this drawing. You are to draw a roof framing plan for an L-shaped ranch home that has the following exterior dimensions:

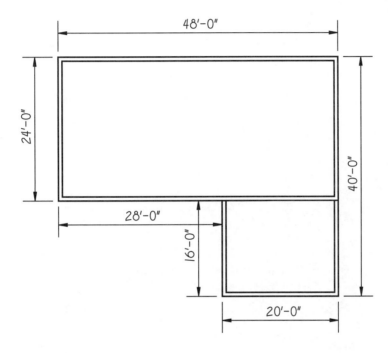

Use C-size paper and a scale of 1/4″ = 1′-0″. Include the following elements in your design:
> Use 2″ × 4″ engineered wood roof trusses that have a pitch of 5:12 and 24″OC spacing.
> Plan the roof framing for a gable roof with 24″ overhangs on all sides.
> The bottom chords of the trusses should be horizontal from fascia to fascia to allow for 12″ insulation in the attic.
> Frame an opening for a 16″ × 16″ chimney that pierces the roof between two trusses.
> Draw a large-scale detail of a typical roof truss to be used to span the 20′ wide section. Show dimensions.
> Include a note that bracing should be per code and sheathing is 1/2″ CDX plywood.

ROOF FRAMING PLAN	NAME:	19-4

Elevations

20

Name _____

Course _____ Date _____ Score _____

Part I: Completion
Complete each sentence with the proper response. Place your answer on the space provided.

1. The term "elevation" usually refers to the exterior elevations. Interior elevations are generally referred to as _____.

   1. _____

2. Two methods of elevation identification are acceptable. The first method identifies elevations by structure side (front, rear, right side, and left side). The second method identifies elevations by compass points (north, south, east, and west). Identification by _____ is more widely used.

   2. _____

3. The grade line is a very important feature of any exterior elevation. All parts of the structure below this line are shown as _____ lines.

   3. _____

4. The floor area of an attached garage should be at least _____ lower than the interior floor.

   4. _____

5. The linetype (symbol) used to show the location of the finished floor and ceiling on an elevation is usually a _____.

   5. _____

6. An exterior elevation is generated from two drawings—the floor plan and a _____.

   6. _____

7. The fractional pitch or slope triangle may be used to illustrate the roof pitch. However, the _____ method is the preferred method.

   7. _____

8. Notes typically found on a(n) _____ drawing include grade information, exterior wall material notes, roof covering material details, fascia material, and flashing material.

   8. _____

9. The usual scale of a residential exterior elevation is _____.

   9. _____

10. The exterior walls are drawn on the elevation using the _____ plan as a guide.

    10. _____

11. The _____ lines of walls, windows and doors, etc., are drawn in after the vertical lines have been drawn.

11. _____

12. After examining the elevation drawing carefully for completeness and accuracy, the title block and _____ are added.

12. _____

Part II: Short Answer/Listing
Provide brief answers to the following questions.

1. An elevation is usually drawn for each side of the dwelling. What purpose do these elevations serve? _____

_____

_____

2. There are a number of features that should be indicated on an elevation. The primary feature is identification of the side of the house. Name four other features._____

_____

_____

3. Two methods of measuring floor to ceiling height are: finished-floor-to-finished-ceiling distance and the construction dimension. Explain both methods and indicate the one carpenters prefer. _____

Finished-floor-to-finished-ceiling distance: _____

_____

_____

_____

Construction dimension:_____

_____

_____

_____

4. Most building codes specify that the top of the foundation wall be at least 8″ above the grade. Why is this requirement important? _____

_____

5. The placement of windows on an elevation is obtained from the floor plan. How is the vertical height determined? _____

_____

_____

6. On an elevation, gable ends are drawn to indicate the height of the roof. If the dwelling has more than one roof height, which is drawn first?_____

7. The following steps should be used to draw a gable end. Place them in the proper order by labeling them A through E, where A is the first step.

Lay out the desired slope starting from the top-inside corner of the wall plate. A line from this point to the ridge will determine the underside. Note: A variation of this procedure will be necessary for certain roof trusses.

_____

Measure the amount of desired overhang. Do not forget to add the thickness of roof sheathing.

_____

Repeat the procedure for the other side of the roof.

_____

Locate the top of the upper wall plate and the center-line of the proposed ridge location. The ridge is usually in the center between the exterior walls.

_____

Measure the width of the rafter perpendicular to the bottom edge and draw the top edge parallel to the bottom edge of the rafter.

_____

8. Vertical dimensions are generally placed on the elevation drawing. List four vertical dimensions that should be included. _____

_____

_____

9. At what point should the dimensions, notes, and symbols be added to the elevation?

_____

Part III: Multiple Choice

Select the best answer and write the corresponding letter in the space provided.

1. The existing grade line for each outside wall may be obtained from the:

1. _____

   A. Site or floor plan.
   B. Plot or site plan.
   C. Floor or plot plan.
   D. Foundation plan.

2. Ceiling heights of basements should be at least 6'-2" high, while 8'-0" is preferred. Garages must have a ceiling height of at least:

2. _____

   A. 8'-0"
   B. 8'-6"
   C. 9'-0"
   D. 9'-6"

3. _____ lines are used on the elevation to indicate visible wall corners.

    A. Hidden
    B. Construction
    C. Object
    D. Guide

3. _____

4. Window details should be shown on the elevation. The swing and the _____ should be shown on hinged windows.

    A. brick mold or window trim
    B. glass elevation symbol
    C. identification symbols for windows and doors
    D. All of the above.

4. _____

5. A number of symbols are normally shown on an elevation. Generally, the front elevation shows more than the other elevations. From the list of symbols below, which symbol is *always* placed on an elevation drawing?

    A. Exterior wall covering symbol.
    B. Roof pitch symbol.
    C. Window swing symbol.
    D. Cutting plane symbol.

5. _____

6. The roof elements and wall height are important features of the elevation drawing. The _____ supplies the measurements for these two features.

    A. floor plan
    B. section drawing
    C. foundation plan
    D. plot plan

6. _____

7. Any changes to be made in the elevation should be done:

    A. After the dimensions, notes, and symbols have been added.
    B. At any time.
    C. Before the features have been darkened.
    D. After the vertical and horizontal lines have been drawn and the features have been darkened.

7. _____

Part IV: Problems/Activities

1.

Directions:
Draw an elevation view of each of the exterior wall materials indicated below. Symbols should be drawn at 1/4″ = 1′-0″ scale.

BRICK

CONCRETE BLOCK

HORIZONTAL SIDING

VERTICAL SIDING

STUCCO

RUBBLE STONE

CAST CONCRETE

GLASS PANEL

ASHLAR STONE

12″ CERAMIC TILE

EXTERIOR ELEVATION SYMBOLS	NAME:	20-1

2.

Complete the partial front elevation of the two-story colonial below. See Figures 20-1 and 20-2 for ideas.

SCALE: 1/4"=1'-0"

COLONIAL HOUSE ELEVATION | NAME: | 20-2

3.

Directions:

Draw a complete front elevation for the garden house shown below using the following information: thickened-edge slab 24" deep, floor-to-ceiling height of 8'-0", 6'-10" to top of windows and doors, 12" overhang with bottom of soffit level with finished ceiling (truss construction), floor 4" above the grade, 12:12 roof slope asphalt shingles, 6" fascia, vertical siding (rough sawn 12" boards with 1" channel), four-panel doors. Follow the procedure described in Chapter 20 in the text.

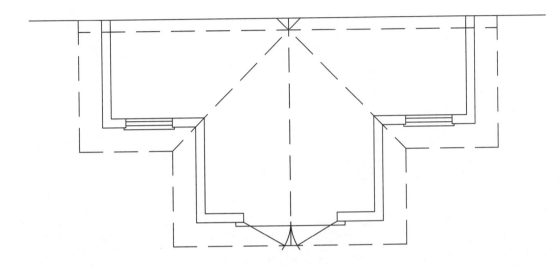

GRADE

SCALE: 1/4"=1'-0"

| GARDEN HOUSE ELEVATION | NAME: | 20-3 |

4. **Front Elevation:** This assignment will be evaluated based on the following factors: Quality of work, use of proper symbols, good dimensioning, an accurate solution, and overall communication provided.

Directions: Study Chapter 20 in your text before attempting this drawing. You are to draw the front elevation for the ranch style home that you designed for Problem/Activity 18-3. Follow the procedure for drawing an exterior elevation presented in the text. Be sure your solution includes the following.

- Scale of the drawing is 1/4″ = 1′-0″.

- Use C-size paper.

- Standard ceiling height of 8′-0″.

- Typical crawl space of at least 18″ and footing below the average maximum frost penetration depth for your area.

- At least a 5:12 roof pitch with asphalt shingles.

- Grade line, floor level, and ceiling levels shown using the proper symbols.

- Proper exterior symbols and recommended height dimensions; 6′-10″ to the top of windows.

- Flashing, gable vents, etc., as required for your house.

Text, Pages 449–463

Name _____

Course _____ Date _____ Score _____

Part I: Multiple Choice
Select the best answer and write the corresponding letter in the space provided.

1. To install 240 volt overhead service to a residence, plan to have _____ wires between the service drop and service head.

    A. 1
    B. 2
    C. 3
    D. 4

1. _____

2. Recommended wire size for branch lighting circuits is:

    A. Number 6
    B. Number 8
    C. Number 10
    D. Number 12

2. _____

3. The overcurrent protection devices most commonly used in residential construction today are:

    A. Fuses
    B. Circuit breakers
    C. Volts
    D. Amperes

3. _____

4. Lighting circuits provide electricity for _____ volt devices such as lamps, radios, and televisions.

    A. 120
    B. 140
    C. 240
    D. None of the above.

4. _____

5. Special appliance circuits normally require Number 12 wire with 20 amp overcurrent protection. Each circuit can supply _____ watts.

    A. 120
    B. 240
    C. 2400
    D. All of the above.

5. _____

6. An individual appliance circuit should be used:

   A. For an appliance that uses a large amount of electricity.
   B. For any 120 volt permanently connected appliance rated over 1,400 watts.
   C. For any 120 volt permanently connected appliance with an automatically starting electric motor.
   D. All of the above.

6. _____

7. Convenience outlets are typically placed 12″ or 18″ above the floor and are spaced approximately _____ apart.

   A. 4′
   B. 8′
   C. 12′
   D. 16′

7. _____

8. Devices that continually monitor the amount of current going to the load and compare it to that coming back are:

   A. Circuit breakers
   B. Fuses
   C. Ground-fault circuit interrupters
   D. All of the above

8. _____

9. A three-way switch is switched from _____ locations.

   A. 1
   B. 2
   C. 3
   D. 4

9. _____

10. Low voltage lighting systems are usually _____ volts.

   A. 24
   B. 14
   C. 12
   D. None of the above.

10. _____

Part II: Short Answer/Listing
Provide brief answers to the following questions.

1. Recommended service entrance voltage is 240 volts. How many voltages are typically available from this voltage and what are they?_____

2. If too small of wire is used in the electrical system, resistance is increased and electricity is wasted. What other situation may occur? _____

3. What mechanism is used to shut off current to the house? _____

_____

Name _____

4. A primary reason for using branch circuits in residential construction is to allow smaller circuit breakers or fuses and wires to keep costs at a minimum and provide ease of handling. Name two other reasons to have branch circuits. _____

_____

_____

5. List three appliances or equipment items in the home that require individual appliance circuits. _____

_____

_____

6. Calculate the recommended number of lighting circuits required for a house that is 40′ × 56′. Allow one lighting circuit for each 400 square feet. _____

_____

7. Calculate the amperage of the service required for a house measuring 40′ × 50′. To determine the size of electrical service entrance, the size of the house, lighting, and appliances should be considered. Also, consider the type and number of branch circuits. Use the minimum code requirement of 3 watts per square foot to calculate the lighting circuits. Allow a minimum of two special appliance circuits for the kitchen and one special appliance circuit for the workshop. The appliances to include are an electric range with oven, refrigerator, washer, electric dryer, dishwasher, garbage disposal, furnace, and a 2000 watt water heater. Refer to the chart in the text for appliance electrical requirements. _____

_____

_____

8. How are electrical boxes used in an electrical system? _____

_____

9. Name two areas of the home where three-way switches are convenient. _____

_____

_____

Part III: Completion
Complete each sentence with the proper response. Place your answer on the space provided.

1. A _____ head should be used when the service entrance equipment is placed along the eaves line.

1. _____

2. The National Electrical Code recommends that a minimum of 100 amp service be supplied to all residences. However, a designer may request as much as _____ amp service to allow for future requirements.

2. _____

3. A workshop would require special _____ circuits above the workbench for hand drills, electric screwdrivers, or soldering irons.

3. _____

4. Number 12 copper wire and _____ amp overcurrent protection is commonly used for most branch circuits in homes built today.

4. _____

5. Some appliances require _____ volt circuits while others require _____volt circuits. Always check the rating of the appliance to determine which circuit is needed.

5. _____

_____

6. Convenience outlets that are _____ should be placed on each exterior wall for work or play activities.

6. _____

7. Switches are placed _____ above the floor; however, a height of _____ to _____ may be more convenient for a person in a wheelchair.

7. _____

_____

_____

8. Locate switches in the bathroom out of reach of the _____ and _____.

8. _____

_____

9. A type of switch that permits the light to be adjusted to the desired brightness is a _____ switch.

9. _____

Part IV: Matching

Match the correct term with its description listed below. Place the corresponding letter on the space provided.

A. Ampere
B. Circuit
C. Circuit breaker or fuse
D. Conductor
E. Convenience outlet or receptacle
F. Lighting outlet
G. Ohm

H. Service drop
I. Service entrance
J. Service panel
K. Voltage
L. Voltage drop
M. Watt

1. The path of electricity that flows from the source to one or more outlets and then back to the source.

1. _____

2. One amp under one volt of pressure.

2. _____

3. Unit of current used to measure the amount of electricity flowing through a conductor per unit of time.

3. _____

4. A safety device that opens an electric circuit if overloaded.

4. _____

5. The force that causes current to move through a wire.

5. _____

6. The unit of measured resistance.

6. _____

7. Conductors and fittings that bring electricity to the dwelling.

7. _____

8. The main distribution box that receives the electricity and distributes it to various parts of the house.

8. _____

9. Material that allows the flow of electricity.

9. _____

Name _____

10. Service conductors from the power lines to the point of attachment to the structure.

11. An outlet designed to provide use of a lighting fixture.

12. A device connected to a circuit to permit electricity to be drawn off for appliances.

13. Condition caused by increased distance from the transformer.

10. _____

11. _____

12. _____

13. _____

Part V: Problems/Activities

1.

Directions:
Label each of the electrical circuits below as to wire size, voltage, and amperage (overcurrent protection). See the completed example for format.

LIGHTING CIRCUIT
12 WIRE, 120 VOLTS, 20 AMPS

SPECIAL APPLIANCE CIRCUIT
_____

REFRIGERATOR
_____

WASHER
_____

DISHWASHER
_____

GARBAGE DISPOSAL
_____

FURNACE
_____

ELECTRIC WATER HEATER
_____

ELECTRIC RANGE/OVEN
_____

20,000 BTU WINDOW AIR CONDITIONER
_____

| RESIDENTIAL ELECTRICAL CIRCUITS | NAME: | 21-1 |

Directions:
Plan the location of switches and outlets for each of the situations below.

A. Ceiling outlet fixture with
single-pole switch

B. Ceiling outlet fixture switched
from two locations.

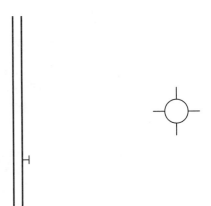

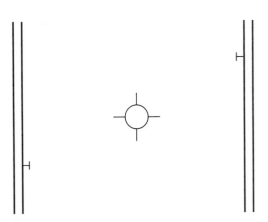

C. Room with switched ceiling outlet fixture and duplex outlets approximately 6 feet apart
along the walls.

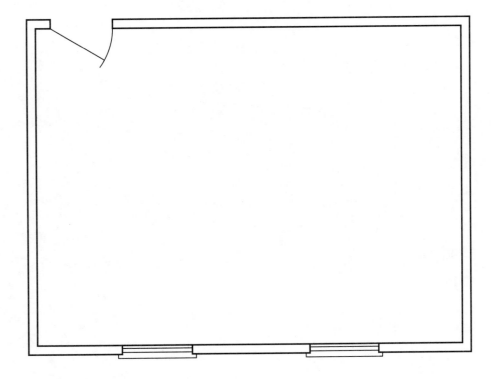

SWITCHES AND OUTLETS	NAME:	21-2

22 Information, Communication, and Security Wiring

Name _____

Course _____ Date _____ Score _____

Part I: Matching
Match the correct term with its description listed below. Place the corresponding letter on the space provided.

A. Cable pair
B. Digital data
C. Hard-wired system
D. RG-6 cable

E. Relays
F. Signaling circuits
G. UTP cable
H. Wiring closet

1. Electrically operated switches.

2. The two wires of a telephone line.

3. A type of coaxial cable.

4. Devices that supply the electrical power to doorbells, chimes, signal lights, or warning devices.

5. More likely to be used in commercial security and surveillance applications than in home systems.

6. Has eight conductors of Number 24 wire bundled inside a PVC jacket.

7. Commonly described as "1s and 0s."

8. The central hub of a structured wiring installation.

1. _____

2. _____

3. _____

4. _____

5. _____

6. _____

7. _____

8. _____

Part II: Completion
Complete each sentence with the proper response. Place your answer on the space provided.

1. Devices that perform _____ functions alert the home owner or a home security agency to potential dangers.

2. Movement of an intruder in the home may be detected by a _____ detector.

3. A home security system in which all doors and windows are wired with magnetic switches inside the frame is called a _____ system.

1. _____

2. _____

3. _____

4. A _____ technology system sends home automation signals over existing electrical wiring to control electrical devices.

4. _____

5. A _____ wiring system provides for complete home security and home automation in one package.

5. _____

6. Bells, buzzers, and chimes usually require between 6 and _____ volts.

6. _____

7. An RJ-11 jack is a type of _____ jack.

7. _____

8. The pin colors for T568A and T568B standards are identical except that pins _____ and _____ are reversed.

8. _____

_____

9. The cable used for cable TV, digital cable, cable modems, and in-home security cameras is _____ cable.

9. _____

10. Most security system consoles have a _____ that permits a silent alarm to be sent to a monitoring station or to set off an audible alarm siren.

10. _____

11. The ability of products to "talk" and "listen" to one another in a home automation system is provided by a _____.

11. _____

Part III: Multiple Choice
Select the best answer and write the corresponding letter in the space provided.

1. Which of the following types of telephone wire requires a special tool to install it?

1. _____

   A. Solid
   B. Stranded
   C. Spiral ribbon
   D. None of the above.

2. What is the maximum length of cable for a run of Category 5 cable for reliable performance?

2. _____

   A. 185 feet
   B. 285 feet
   C. 385 feet
   D. 485 feet

3. Devices that perform _____ functions examine certain aspects of the house to determine their status.

3. _____

   A. programming
   B. switching
   C. communication/recording
   D. None of the above.

4. What type of jacks and plugs are used with Category 5 cable?

    A. RJ-6
    B. RJ-11
    C. RJ-30
    D. RJ-45

4. _____

5. In low-voltage switching, switch conductors carry _____ volts provided by a transformer.

    A. 6
    B. 12
    C. 18
    D. 24

5. _____

6. How many different classes of signaling circuits does the National Electrical Code specify?

    A. One
    B. Two
    C. Three
    D. Four

6. _____

Part IV: Problems/Activities

1.

Directions:
Draw each of the symbols specified below as shown in the completed example.
Scale is 1/4" = 1'-0".

[A]

| AUDIO OUTLET | MOTION DETECTOR | FLOOR OUTLET |

| VIDEO OUTLET | DOOR ALARM | DATA OUTLET |

| FIRE ALARM | SMOKE DETECTOR | INTERCOM |

| FIRE HORN | THERMAL SENSOR | JUNCTION BOX |

| DISCONNECT SWITCH | SECURITY KEY PAD | GFCI OUTLET |

| TRANSFORMER | SPRINKLER | SPEAKER OUTLET |

| SECURITY SYMBOLS | NAME: | 22-1 |

2. Select one of the floor plans in the textbook, one provided by your instructor, or one of your own and plan the location of each component for a home security and automation system. Draw the plan using manual or CADD methods. Draw the plan at 1/4″ = 1′-0″ scale and select an appropriate size drawing sheet.

The Electrical Plan
23

Text, Pages 483–490

Name _____

Course _____ Date _____ Score _____

Part I: Short Answer/Listing
Provide brief answers to the following questions.

1. What is the purpose of an electrical plan? _____

   _____

   _____

2. List at least five items commonly shown on an electrical plan. _____

   _____

   _____

   _____

   _____

3. A home may require several different types of switches. Which type of switch is generally the least expensive and most popular? _____

   _____

4. Most rooms are more functional when a switched outlet is included. How does a switched outlet differ from a regular outlet? _____

   _____

   _____

5. Name at least one area where each of the following types of lighting are used.

   Ceiling fixtures: _____

   Fluorescent lights: _____

   Recessed lighting fixtures: _____

6. Where should the amperage rating of the service required be shown on the electrical plan?

   _____

7. Identify the electrical symbols indicated on the partial electrical plan shown below.

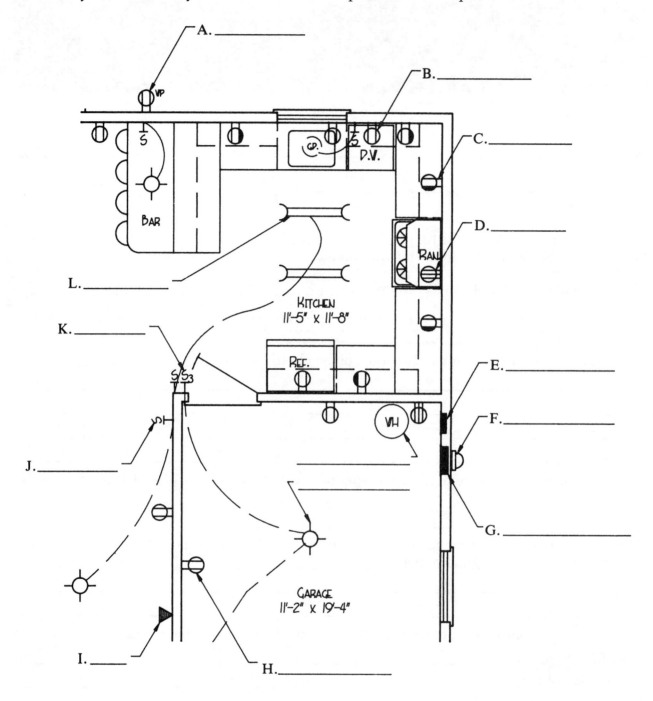

A. _____

B. _____

C. _____

D. _____

E. _____

F. _____

G. _____

L. _____

K. _____

J. _____

I. _____

H. _____

Part II: Completion
Complete each sentence with the proper response. Place your answer on the space provided.

1. The electrical plan is a _____ view section drawing.

1. _____

2. The _____ requires that the service entrance equipment be located as close as practical to the point where the wires attach to the house.

2. _____

Name _____

3. _____ patterns should be considered when locating switches to control lighting fixtures and convenience outlets.

3. _____

4. Most convenience outlets have _____ receptacles.

4. _____

5. The two different types of lights commonly used in the home are incandescent and _____.

5. _____

6. The number of_____, special appliance, and individual appliance circuits should be indicated on the electrical plan.

6. _____

Part III: Multiple Choice

Select the best answer and write the corresponding letter in the space provided.

1. The electrical plan is normally traced from the:

   A. Elevations.
   B. Floor plan.
   C. Plot plan.
   D. None of the above.

1. _____

2. It is better to locate the service entrance near the area that uses the greatest amount of electricity because:

   A. It is less expensive and more efficient.
   B. It is a requirement of the utility company.
   C. None of the above.
   D. All of the above.

2. _____

3. On the electrical plan, a _____ connects the switch to the fixture, outlet, or appliance it operates.

   A. border line drawn freehand
   B. construction line drawn with a straightedge
   C. hidden line or centerline drawn with an irregular curve
   D. All of the above.

3. _____

4. Lighting fixtures used to provide lighting for areas such as walks, patios, and drives should be:

   A. Recessed fixtures.
   B. Fluorescent fixtures.
   C. Interior fixtures.
   D. Exterior fixtures.

4. _____

5. The specifications for each lighting fixture are usually listed on the:

   A. Lighting fixture schedule.
   B. Floor plan.
   C. Elevations.
   D. None of the above.

5. _____

Part IV: Problems/Activities

1.

Directions:
Draw each of the electrical symbols specified below as shown in the completed example.
Scale is 1/4" = 1'-0".

CEILING OUTLET FIXTURE	RECESSED OUTLET FIXTURE	FAN HANGER OUTLET
JUNCTION BOX	DUPLEX RECEPTACLE OUTLET	QUADRUPLEX RECEPTACLE OUTLET
SPLIT–WIRED DUPLEX RECEPTACLE OUTLET	SPECIAL PURPOSE SINGLE RECEPTACLE OUTLET	WEATHERPROOF DUPLEX OUTLET
240 VOLT OUTLET	SINGLE-POLE SWITCH	THREE–WAY SWITCH
PUSH BUTTON	CHIMES	DIMMER SWITCH
THERMOSTAT	TELEPHONE	FLUORESCENT FIXTURE

ELECTRICAL SYMBOLS	NAME:	23-1

2.

Directions:
Using the garage floor plan below, prepare an electrical plan that includes the following features:
> Three-way switch for two ceiling outlet fixtures.
> Switch for two outside lights on either side of the garage door.
> Four duplex outlets on garage side walls (two each side).
> Two duplex outlets above the workbench.
> Garage door opener outlet and switch.

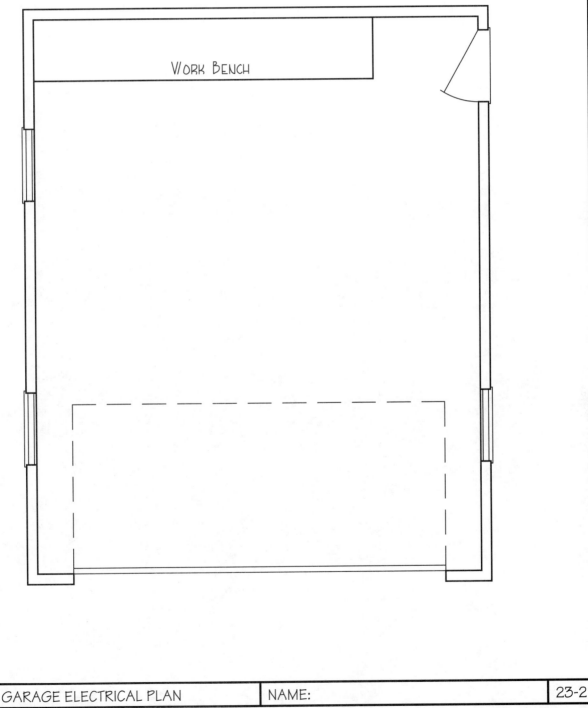

WORK BENCH

GARAGE ELECTRICAL PLAN	NAME:	23-2

3. **Electrical Plan.** Draw an **electrical plan for the ranch house you designed for Problem 3** of Chapter 18. Be sure to follow the procedures described in Chapter 23 for drawing an electrical plan. Your plan will be evaluated on the proper use of symbols, application of principles discussed in the text, functional electrical layout, and quality of work. Use C-size paper and 1/4" = 1'-0" scale.

Residential Plumbing
24

Text, Pages 491–504

Name _____

Course _____ Date _____ Score _____

Part I: Matching
Match the correct term with its description listed below. Place the corresponding letter on the space provided.

A. Branch main
B. Building main
C. Cleanout
D. Hot water branch
E. House sewer
F. Percolation test

G. Main stacks
H. Secondary stacks
I. Stack wall
J. Sump
K. Vent stack

1. Water pipe that enters the house from a water source.

1. _____

2. Connects the hot water main (from water heater) to each fixture.

2. _____

3. Stacks with water closets draining into them.

3. _____

4. Stacks that do not drain water closets.

4. _____

5. Connects the fixture to the stack in the water and waste removal system.

5. _____

6. Exterior part of the house drain.

6. _____

7. Provides for using a cable to dislodge waste in the house drain.

7. _____

8. Permits air into the drainage system.

8. _____

9. Provides space for the soil and stack vent.

9. _____

10. Tile or concrete pit.

10. _____

11. Soil test to determine suitability of soil for a disposal field.

11. _____

Part II: Completion
Complete each sentence with the proper response. Place your answer on the space provided.

1. _____ devices are usually installed after a branch line is provided for hose bibs and before the main line is divided into the cold water and hot water lines.

1. _____

2. When large pipes must pass through a joist, the joist should be _____ to strengthen the member.

2. _____

3. A single fixture may be isolated from the water supply system by a _____ valve.

3. _____

4. Hot and cold water lines often run parallel to each other. Some form of insulating material should be used if they are placed closer than _____ to each other.

4. _____

5. Drain pipes generally are smooth inside with few projections or sharp _____.

5. _____

6. The _____ stacks and _____ stacks empty into the house drain.

6. _____

_____

7. A septic tank and _____ field are the two basic elements of a private sewage disposal system.

7. _____

8. Frequently, the number of _____ in a home is used as an indication of the size septic tank required.

8. _____

9. The drain field lines are laid almost level and approximately _____ below the ground surface.

9. _____

Part III: Short Answer/Listing
Provide brief answers to the following questions.

1. List the three main parts of the residential plumbing system. _____

_____

_____

2. What are two steps that can be taken when installing water pipes in cold climates to prevent freezing of the pipes? _____

_____

_____

3. Generally, underground water supply lines are which type of pipe? _____

_____

_____

4. What are on-demand water heaters? _____

_____

5. How many fixtures can be drained into a single main drain? _____

_____

6. How does the plumbing system provide for gas removal? _____

_____

_____

7. Name the two functions that the septic tank performs. _____

_____

_____

Name _____

8. What is the function of the disposal field?_____

_____

_____

9. Calculate the required size in square feet of a disposal field for a three-bedroom home. The disposal field will be a continuous bed and laid in poor soil (percolation rate of 35 minutes per inch). Refer to the chart in Figure 24-18 in the text. _____

_____

Part IV: Multiple Choice

Select the best answer and write the corresponding letter in the space provided.

1. Branch lines:

   A. Are smaller than main lines.
   B. Are larger than main lines.
   C. Cannot supply more than one fixture.
   D. Are shared between the cold and hot water mains.

1. _____

2. Copper tubing is commonly used for water supply systems. Main lines are usually at least _____ in diameter.

   A. 1/2″
   B. 3/4″
   C. 1″
   D. 1-1/4″

2. _____

3. Air compression chambers are installed at faucets to:

   A. Shut off the water supply to the faucet.
   B. Remove gas from the branch line.
   C. Increase the water flow.
   D. Cushion the water flow and reduce pipe noise during use.

3. _____

4. The waste removal or drainage system uses _____ to carry the waste to the sewer.

   A. pressure
   B. air flow
   C. gravity
   D. All of the above.

4. _____

5. Drains are usually _____ in diameter to prevent solids from accumulating at any point within the system.

   A. 2″
   B. 4″
   C. 6″
   D. None of the above.

5. _____

6. The most obvious parts of the plumbing system are the
   _____, which include sinks, bathtubs, and water
   closets.

   A. appliances
   B. fixtures
   C. Both A and B.
   D. None of the above.

6. _____

7. A lot size of at least _____ is recommended for a house
   with a private sewage disposal system.

   A. 1 acre
   B. 1-1/2 acres
   C. 2 acres
   D. 3 acres

7. _____

8. The minimum size of a septic tank should be _____
   gallons.

   A. 250
   B. 500
   C. 750
   D. 1000

8. _____

9. The disposal field should be located downhill from the:

   A. Driveway.
   B. Parking lot.
   C. Water supply well.
   D. All of the above.

9. _____

Directions:
Using the simplified house section below, draw the schematic of a residential water supply system. Connect each fixture to the cold water and hot water mains (where appropriate). Complete the system to the building main. Label each pipe as to size and name. Include shutoff valves for each branch line and fixture. Provide a hose bib and air chamber at each faucet. See Figure 24-1 in the text for a typical layout.

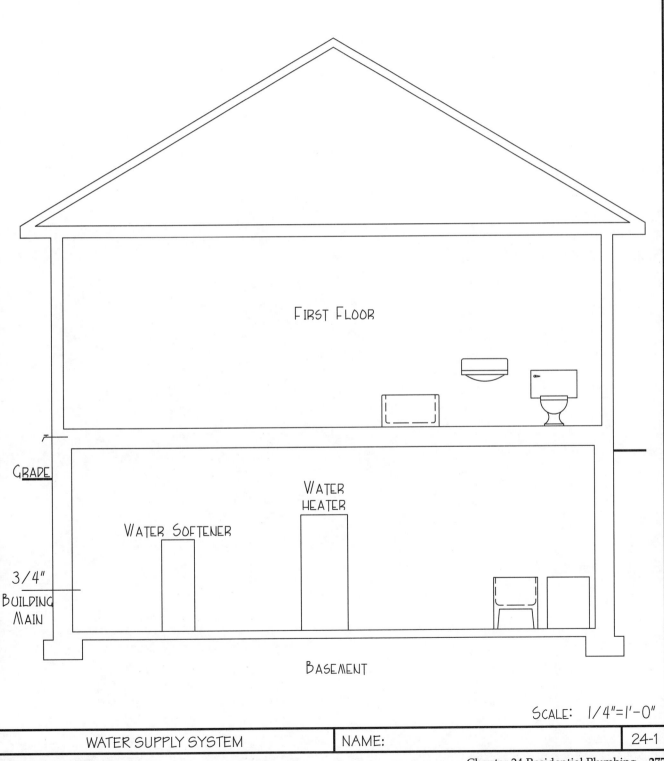

FIRST FLOOR

GRADE

WATER HEATER

WATER SOFTENER

3/4"
BUILDING
MAIN

BASEMENT

SCALE: 1/4"=1'-0"

WATER SUPPLY SYSTEM   NAME: 24-1

2.

Directions:
Using the simplified house section below, draw the schematic of a residential water and waste removal system. Connect each fixture to the house drain and connect the house drain to the house sewer. Provide a 4" vent stack through the roof and label each part of the system showing size of pipe used. Study Figure 24-8 in your text for a layout. Remember, this is a gravity system.

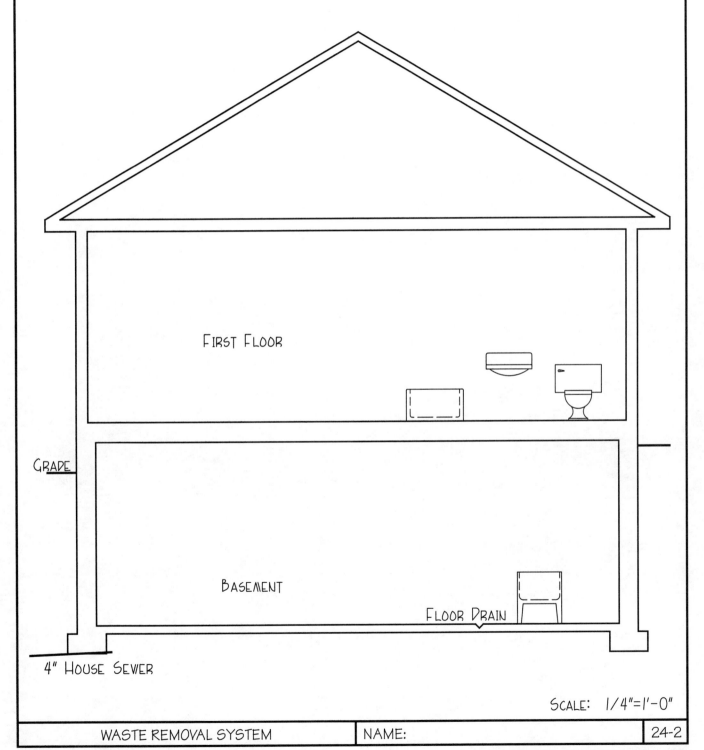

FIRST FLOOR

GRADE

BASEMENT

FLOOR DRAIN

4" HOUSE SEWER

SCALE: 1/4"=1'-0"

| WASTE REMOVAL SYSTEM | NAME: | 24-2 |

3.

Directions:
Suppose you purchased Lot #2 in the subdivision below and wish to install a private well for household use. The surrounding lots have wells and septic systems already and your lot has the septic tank and disposal field in place. The local code specifies a minimum distance of 150′ from the disposal field and 75′ from the septic tank to the well. Indicate the area on your lot where the well can be placed.

SCALE: 1″=50′-0″

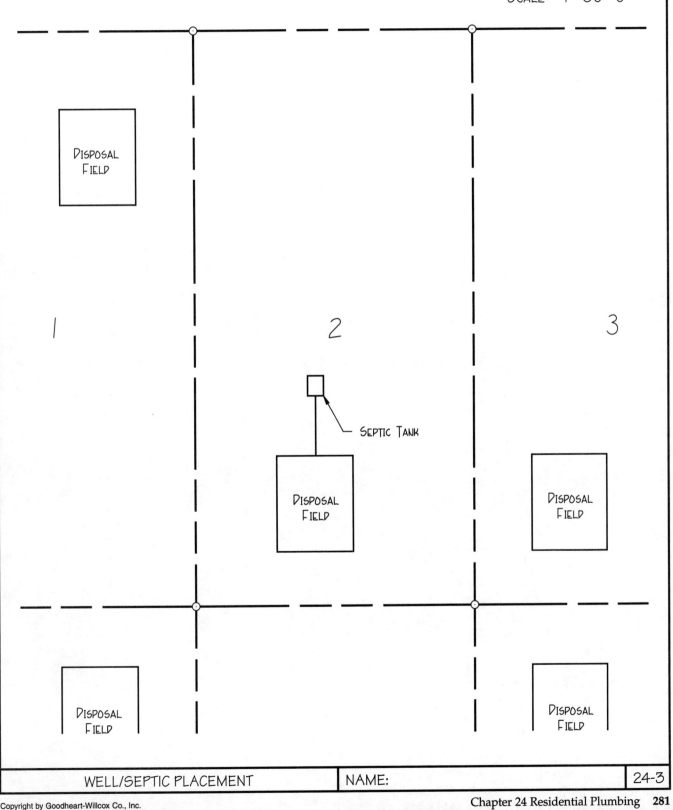

| WELL/SEPTIC PLACEMENT | NAME: | 24-3 |

The Plumbing Plan

25

Text, Pages 505–514

Name _____

Course _____ Date _____ Score _____

Part I: Completion
Complete each sentence with the proper response. Place your answer on the space provided.

1. The plumbing plan is a _____ view drawing that shows the complete plumbing system.

2. The plumbing plan should be coordinated with the _____ and climate control systems.

3. The slope of waste lines, usually _____ inches per foot, should be shown on the plumbing plan.

4. The width of lines drawn for waste lines should be _____ than that used for lines representing water supply lines.

5. Each fixture in the water supply system should have a _____ valve.

6. Type _____ copper pipe is a medium weight pipe often used for interior hot and cold installations.

7. Information on exact plumbing fixtures to be used in the structure may be obtained from _____ catalogs.

8. The position of the water softener, filter, and water storage tank should be shown on the plumbing plan along the _____.

9. Floor drains are usually connected to the _____ or a dry well.

10. The copper tubing designation DWV refers to _____.

1. _____

2. _____

3. _____

4. _____

5. _____

6. _____

7. _____

8. _____

9. _____

10. _____

Part II: Short Answer/Listing
Provide brief answers to the following questions.

1. List the features commonly shown on a plumbing plan. _____

_____

_____

_____

_____

2. Where should hose bibs and fixtures that do not need filtered or softened water be connected?

_____

_____

_____

3. How many plumbing plans will a two-story house require? _____

_____

4. What does the National Plumbing Code require with regard to the location of fixtures?

_____

_____

5. What does the "nominal diameter" of a pipe mean? _____

_____

6. A plumbing fixture schedule is a vital part of the plumbing plan. What information is usually given on the schedule? _____

_____

_____

_____

7. Information is often needed to further explain the plumbing plan. This might consist of details about installation procedures, materials, etc. How should this information appear on the plumbing plan? _____

_____

_____

8. To draw attention to plumbing fixtures, what type of line can be used to draw the fixtures?

_____

9. Which of the following symbols should be used on a plumbing plan to indicate a sprinkler line?

9. _____

   A. —— S —— S —— S ——   C. ____ _ _ ____ _ _ __

   B. __ __ __ __ __ __ _   D. ____ __ ____ __ __

10. What does a legend explain on a plumbing plan? _____

_____

Name _____

Part III: Multiple Choice
Select the best answer and write the corresponding letter in the space provided.

1. The plumbing plan is usually traced from the _____.

   A. site plan
   B. floor plan
   C. plot plan
   D. elevations

1. _____

2. The _____ should be planned first as the plumbing system is usually planned around it.

   A. hot water main
   B. cold water main
   C. waste line network
   D. network of fixtures

2. _____

3. The Federal Housing Administration specifies that a lavatory should have at least a _____ size pipe for the water supply line.

   A. 1/4"
   B. 3/8"
   C. 1/2"
   D. 3/4"

3. _____

4. In order to plan the exact location of each fixture, study the _____ plan to determine the location of utilities.

   A. plot
   B. foundation
   C. floor
   D. site

4. _____

5. The symbol shown indicates a _____.

   A. coupling or sleeve
   B. floor drain in a plan view
   C. gate valve
   D. hose bib in a plan view

5. _____

Part IV: Problems/Activities

1.

Directions:
Draw the plan view symbol for each of the plumbing symbols listed below. The scale for these symbols is 1/4" = 1'-0".

SOIL STACK	GATE VALVE	COUPLING OR SLEEVE

ELBOW TURNED UP	ELBOW TURNED DOWN	TEE TURNED UP

METER	HOSE BIB	TEE TURNED DOWN

CLEANOUT	FLOOR DRAIN	TEE HORIZONTAL

×   ×   ×   ×

COLD WATER LINE   GAS LINE

×   ×   ×   ×

HOT WATER LINE   SPRINKLER LINE

×   ×   ×   ×

SOIL OR WASTE LINE   VENT PIPE

PLUMBING SYMBOLS	NAME:	25-1

2.

Directions:
Show the typical piping arrangement for the two situations below. Use proper symbols and show tees, elbows, etc.

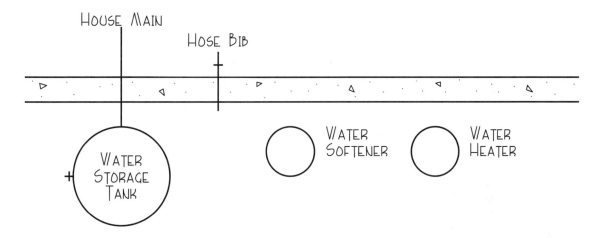

HOUSE MAIN

HOSE BIB

WATER
STORAGE
TANK

WATER
SOFTENER

WATER
HEATER

SCALE: 1/4"=1'-0"

WATER SUPPLY LINES

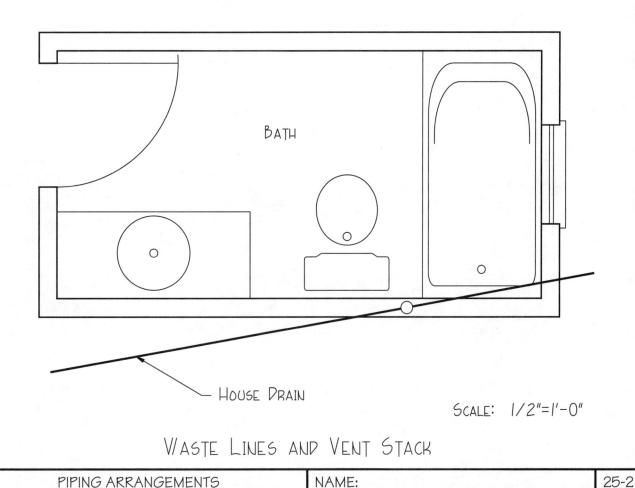

BATH

HOUSE DRAIN

SCALE: 1/2"=1'-0"

WASTE LINES AND VENT STACK

| PIPING ARRANGEMENTS | NAME: | 25-2 |

3.

Directions:
Draw a plumbing plan for the small cottage below. Assume the cottage has its own well and septic system. Use proper symbols and indicate pipe sizes. Use C-size paper and a scale of 1/4" = 1'-0".

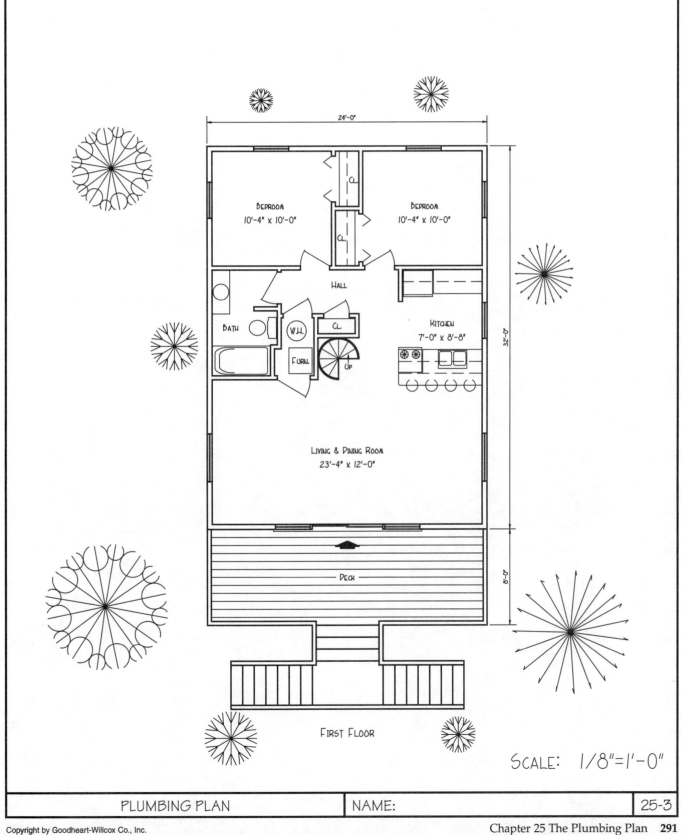

24'-0"

BEDROOM
10'-4" x 10'-0"

CL.

BEDROOM
10'-4" x 10'-0"

CL.

HALL

BATH

W.H.

CL.

KITCHEN
7'-0" x 8'-8"

FURN.

UP

32'-0"

LIVING & DINING ROOM
23'-4" x 12'-0"

DECK

8'-0"

FIRST FLOOR

SCALE: 1/8"=1'-0"

| PLUMBING PLAN | NAME: | 25-3 |

26 Residential Climate Control

Text, Pages 515–537

Name _____

Course _____ Date _____ Score _____

Part I: Short Answer/Listing
Provide brief answers to the following questions.

1. Adequate insulation is important for heating and cooling a home efficiently. Name three areas where insulation should be placed in a home with a crawl space. _____
   _____
   _____

2. Name two areas of the home that should be ventilated to reduce temperature and moisture.
   _____

3. What device is sometimes required to remove moisture from the air?_____

4. List the four types of heating systems._____
   _____
   _____

5. List four advantages of a forced-air system. _____
   _____
   _____
   _____

6. When installing a forced-air system into a large home, what method might you consider to have an effective system? Explain this method. _____
   _____
   _____

7. Of the four types of heating systems, which two might be a logical choice for a dwelling that has natural gas available? _____
   _____

8. If choosing a heating system for a house to be built in Minnesota, which heating system would *not* be a good choice? Why not? _____
   _____

Part II: Multiple Choice
Select the best answer and write the corresponding letter in the space provided.

1. _____ insulation is often used along the foundation wall and perimeter of the floor in houses with slab foundations.

   A. Batt
   B. Loose fill
   C. Rigid foam
   D. All of the above.

   1. _____

2. In residential home construction, use _____ to provide shade and block cold winter winds.

   A. weatherstripping
   B. landscaping
   C. overhangs
   D. None of the above.

   2. _____

3. _____ are used to increase the amount of moisture in the air.

   A. Humidifiers
   B. Dehumidifiers
   C. Air cleaners
   D. All of the above.

   3. _____

4. A(n) _____ warms the air in a furnace and moves it to various areas of the house through ducts.

   A. electric radiant system
   B. forced-air system
   C. hydronic system
   D. heat pump

   4. _____

5. A device that automatically activates the heating or cooling system when the temperature in the house reaches a predetermined level is a:

   A. thermostat
   B. cupola vent
   C. plenum
   D. All of the above.

   5. _____

6. The _____ system is a type of hydronic system commonly used in residential construction.

   A. counterflow
   B. upflow
   C. one-pipe
   D. None of the above.

   6. _____

Name _____

7. One advantage of a hydronic heating system is that:

    A. The temperature of each room can be controlled individually.
    B. Adequate amounts of heat are provided quickly.
    C. Central air conditioning may be added to the system.
    D. All of the above.

7. _____

8. The disadvantage(s) of an electric radiant system include:

    A. Slow recovery after a sudden drop in temperature.
    B. No provision for humidification, air filtration, or cooling.
    C. Both A and B.
    D. None of the above.

8. _____

9. A(n) _____ removes heat from the air and pumps the heat into the house to heat it or pumps it from the house to cool it.

    A. forced-air system
    B. hydronic system
    C. electric radiant system
    D. heat pump

9. _____

10. Programmable thermostats have a(n) _____ and can automatically control your home's heating and cooling systems.

    A. mercury switch
    B. microprocessor
    C. telephone port
    D. satellite connection

10. _____

Part III: Completion

Complete each sentence with the proper response. Place your answer on the space provided.

1. The purpose of _____ is to prevent the transfer of heat or cold from one location to another.

1. _____

2. Three important factors that affect the heating and cooling efficiency of the home are insulation, ventilation, and _____ orientation.

2. _____

3. Warmer air will hold _____ moisture than cooler air.

3. _____

4. _____ devices remove dust and small particles from the air.

4. _____

5. A logical choice of a forced-air furnace for a ranch style house with a crawl space and limited interior space would be a _____ furnace.

5. _____

6. A type of hydronic system suitable for geographical areas with mild temperatures is the _____ system.

6. _____

7. _____ wiring is used in electric radiant systems and placed in the ceiling, floor, or baseboards.

7. _____

8. Air cleaning and humidification are easily added to _____ and forced-air systems.

8. _____

Part IV: Matching
Match the correct term with its description listed below. Place the corresponding letter on the space provided.

A. Btu
B. Design temperature difference
C. Heat loss
D. Infiltration
E. Inside design temperature

F. Outside design temperature
G. Relative humidity
H. Resistivity
I. U factor

1. The ratio of water vapor in the atmosphere to the amount required to saturate it at the same temperature.

1. _____

2. British thermal unit.

2. _____

3. Ability to resist the transfer of heat or cold.

3. _____

4. The number of Btus transmitted in one hour through one square foot of building material for each degree of temperature difference.

4. _____

5. The amount of heat that escapes through exposed surfaces of the dwelling for average temperatures.

5. _____

6. Heat loss through spaces around windows and doors.

6. _____

7. The difference between the outside design temperature and the inside design temperature.

7. _____

8. The preferred room temperature level.

8. _____

9. The average outdoor temperature for the winter months.

9. _____

1.

Directions:
Add insulation to the crawl space/first floor section below to maximize resistance to heat loss. The following areas are suggested for consideration: RF insulation on the outside of the stud wall, batt insulation between the studs and between the floor joists, sill sealer, and RF insulation either inside or outside of the foundation wall.

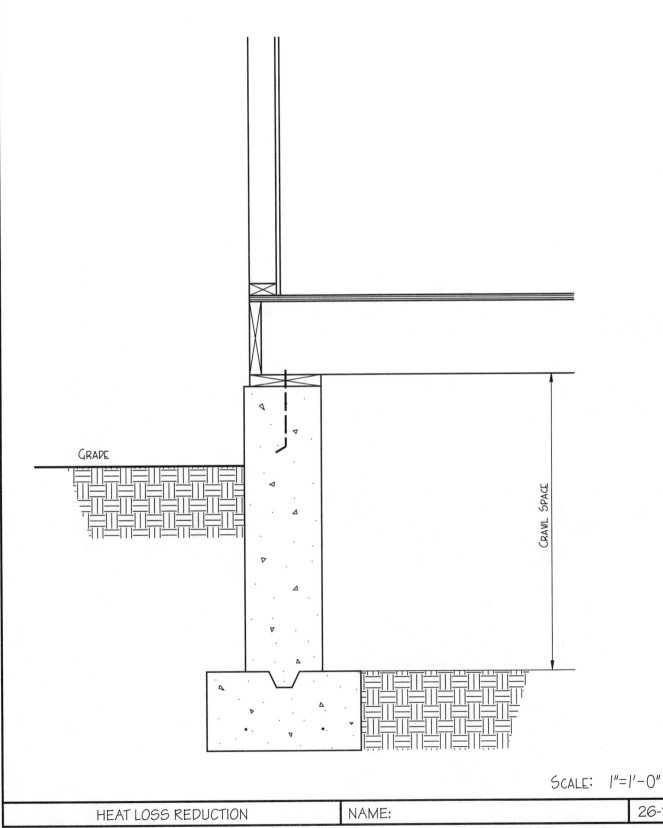

GRADE

CRAWL SPACE

SCALE: 1"=1'-0"

| HEAT LOSS REDUCTION | NAME: | 26-1 |

2.

Directions:
Calculate the heat loss for the exterior wall below and fill in the values as indicated. The wall has no windows or doors.

Wall Area Calculation:
Total wall area = 8'-0" × 12'-0" = _____ square feet
Window and door area = 0 square feet
Net wall area = _____ square feet

Resistivity of Wall Materials:

4" Face brick	=	_____
1" Air space	=	_____
3/4" RF insulation	=	_____
3-1/2" Batt insulation	=	_____
1/2" Drywall	=	_____
Outside air film	=	_____
Inside air film	=	_____
Total resistivity	=	_____

AIR FILM, R = 0.68
1/2" DRYWALL, R = 0.45
3-1/2" BATT INSULATION R = 11.0
3/4" RF INSULATION R = 2.88
1" AIR SPACE, R = 1.01
FACE BRICK, R = 0.45
OUTSIDE AIR FILM R = 0.17

U Factor for Net Wall Area:
1.00 divided by total resistivity = _____
Therefore, U factor for net wall = _____

Design Temperature Difference:

Inside design temperature	=	70°
Outside design temperature	=	5°
Design temperature difference	=	_____

BTU/H for Net Wall:
Net wall area × U factor × temperature difference
_____ square feet × _____ × _____ = _____ BTU/H

Therefore, the heat loss for the 8'-0" × 12'-0" wall is _____ BTU/H.

HEAT LOSS CALCULATIONS	NAME:	26-2

Climate Control Plan

27

Text, Pages 539–547

Name _____

Course _____ Date _____ Score _____

Part I: Multiple Choice
Select the best answer and write the corresponding letter in the space provided.

1. The climate control plan is traced from the _____.

    A. plot plan
    B. foundation plan
    C. floor plan
    D. site plan

1. _____

2. A climate control plan should show information such as:

    A. Electrical outlets and switches.
    B. The location of thermostats and registers or baseboard convectors.
    C. The hot water branch lines to each fixture.
    D. All of the above.

2. _____

3. Which of the following is true of the perimeter system of outlets?

    A. It concentrates heating or cooling along outside walls.
    B. It concentrates heating or cooling along interior walls.
    C. It does not use registers or baseboard units.
    D. All of the above.

3. _____

4. A(n) _____ round duct is generally recommended when the system is to be used for cooling as well as heating.

    A. 6″
    B. 8″
    C. 10″
    D. 12″

4. _____

5. The heat loss for each room should be calculated for a hydronic system to determine:

    A. Whether an extended plenum or radial system should be used.

    B. The size of the baseboard unit or convector cabinet.

    C. The size of pipe to use.

    D. All of the above.

5. _____

Part II: Completion

Complete each sentence with the proper response. Place your answer on the space provided.

1. The climate control plan is a _____ view section drawing.

1. _____

2. The distribution system in a climate control plan usually consists of ducts or _____.

2. _____

3. Two or more outlets should be used for a room that has more than _____ feet of exterior wall.

3. _____

4. The _____ system uses a large rectangular duct for the main supply and round ducts connecting to each register.

4. _____

5. The plenum duct size required to accommodate eight 8″ ducts for heating and cooling is _____.

5. _____

6. Specifications that show equipment to be used in the system may be identified on a climate control equipment _____.

6. _____

7. The cold air return in a forced-air system should be drawn as a _____ line.

7. _____

8. The scale used for drawing the climate control plan is generally _____.

8. _____

Part III: Short Answer/Listing

Provide brief answers to the following questions.

1. List the features typically shown on the climate control plan. _____

_____

_____

_____

_____

2. How are ducts and pipes indicated on the climate control plan? _____

_____

_____

_____

Part IV: Problems/Activities

1.

Directions:
Draw the climate control symbols indicated below. The scale is 1/4″ = 1′-0″.

Warm Air Supply

Cold Air Return

Second Floor Supply

Second Floor Return

12″ x 18″ Duct/Flow

Duct Change in Size

Thermostat   Humidistat   Radiator

Convector   Register   Ceiling Duct Outlet

Scale: 1/4″=1′-0″

| CLIMATE CONTROL SYMBOLS | NAME: | 27-1 |

2.

Directions:
Design a simple heating duct system for the small house below that illustrates the desired distribution of warm air and provides for cold air return. You may assume the extended plenum to be 8″ × 14″ with ducts 6″ in diameter. Remember to provide for cold air return. Study Figure 27-9 in the text. Draw the plan on B-size paper at a scale of 1/4″ = 1'-0″.

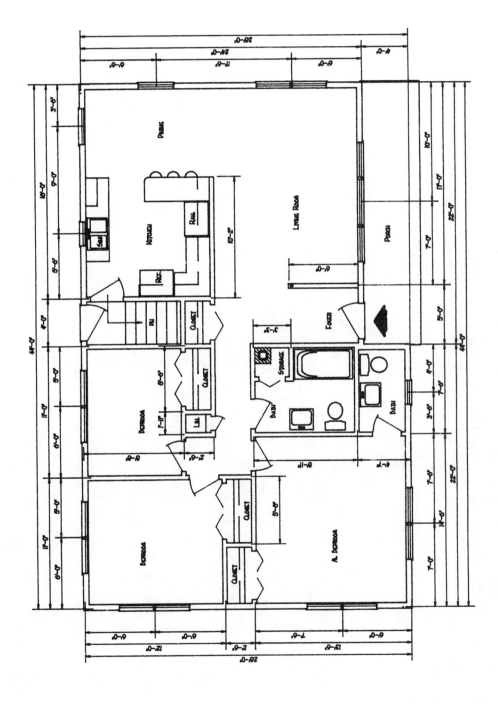

SCALE: 1/8″=1'-0″

| HEATING DUCT SYSTEM | NAME: | 27-2 |

28 Solar Space Heating

Text, Pages 549–562

Name _____

Course _____ Date _____ Score _____

Part I: Completion
Complete each sentence with the proper response. Place your answer on the space provided.

1. Fans and pumps are *not* used in _____ solar space heating systems.

2. _____ gain systems incorporate large areas of south-facing glazing (glass or other material) that permit large amounts of sunlight to enter the interior space of the dwelling to heat the air inside.

3. Masonry walls store heat more efficiently if the insulation is placed on the _____ surface of the wall.

4. Heat is collected and stored outside the living space in a(n) _____ gain system.

5. Pumps, fans, and other devices to distribute heat are required in _____ solar space heating systems.

6. Every solar collector has some type of _____ that is designed to absorb heat from solar radiation.

7. In a warm air system, a well-insulated stone-filled box or crawl space area is often used as a _____.

8. A typical _____ solar system is composed of a bank of collectors, a warm water storage tank, a pump to circulate the water, some form of heat exchange device in the living space, and controls for operating the system.

9. Factors that affect the total Btus that may be produced by a typical solar collector in a specific geographical location include mean solar radiation, total hours of sunshine, and the _____ of the collector.

1. _____

2. _____

3. _____

4. _____

5. _____

6. _____

7. _____

8. _____

9. _____

Part II: Short Answer/Listing

Provide brief answers to the following questions.

1. Name the two basic methods or systems used for solar space heating. _____

_____

2. Why are large thermal masses necessary in a direct gain system? _____

_____

3. What are five disadvantages of a water storage wall?_____

_____

_____

_____

_____

4. List three requirements of a solar greenhouse in order to be efficient in a cold climate.

_____

_____

_____

_____

5. What three features should be present in a good-quality solar collector used for a warm air solar system?_____

_____

_____

6. Generally, what is the most efficient tilt angle for a solar collector? _____

_____

7. In a warm air system, how is heat from the storage area distributed to the living area?

_____

_____

8. Name two concerns to address when considering a warm water solar system.

_____

_____

_____

_____

Name _____

Part III: Multiple Choice
Select the best answer and write the corresponding letter in the space provided.

1. A direct gain system:

    A. Is a popular type of active solar system.
    B. Uses pumps and fans to move the heat.
    C. Is a type of passive solar system.
    D. None of the above.

1. _____

2. Indirect gain systems:

    A. Use a group of solar collectors to collect heat.
    B. Use a large thermal mass located between the sun and living space to collect and store heat.
    C. Are the most popular type of solar heating systems.
    D. All of the above.

2. _____

3. The vents in the Trombe wall should be closed at night during the heating season to prevent:

    A. Reverse thermosiphoning.
    B. Thermosiphoning.
    C. All of the above.
    D. None of the above.

3. _____

4. Advantage(s) of an isolated gain system include:

    A. Little interior space needs to be exposed to the sun.
    B. Little interior space is required for heat collection devices.
    C. Collected heat is easier to control.
    D. All of the above.

4. _____

5. A bank of collectors, a heat storage box, and blowers are required in a:

    A. Warm water system.
    B. Warm air solar system.
    C. Direct gain system.
    D. Indirect gain system.

5. _____

6. The most used material for warm air absorber plates is:

    A. Copper.
    B. Aluminum.
    C. Steel.
    D. Cast iron.

6. _____

7. As a rule, the size of the heat storage for active solar systems should be:

    A. Sufficiently large to store enough heat for three days of cloudy weather.
    B. One-half the size of the collector area.
    C. Twice the size of the collector area.
    D. As large as possible.

7. _____

8. The heated water necessary in the warm water system is usually stored in a(n):

   A. Large tank placed in the attic.
   B. Indoor swimming pool.
   C. Large insulated tank usually located in the basement or crawl space.
   D. None of the above.

8. _____

9. Warm water solar systems heat the air in the living space by:

   A. Absorber plates with copper tubes attached.
   B. Liquid-to-air heat exchangers such as baseboard convectors.
   C. Solar collectors.
   D. All of the above.

9. _____

Part IV: Matching

Match the correct term with its description listed below. Place the corresponding letter on the space provided.

A. Conduction
B. Convection
C. Flat plate collector
D. Glauber's salt
E. Radiation

F. Solar radiation
G. Sun space
H. Thermosiphoning
I. Trombe wall
J. Water storage wall

1. The sun's energy.

1. _____

2. Transfer of heat by moving fluids, such as liquids or gases.

2. _____

3. The flow of heat through an object by the movement of heat from one molecule to another.

3. _____

4. Waves of infrared or invisible light that move heat through space.

4. _____

5. A massive wall colored dark on the outside to absorb heat from the sun.

5. _____

6. The result of a fluid expanding and rising.

6. _____

7. A wall made of water-filled containers capable of storing heat.

7. _____

8. A phase change material that changes from a solid to a liquid as it heats up.

8. _____

9. A solar greenhouse.

9. _____

10. A type of absorber plate.

10. _____

Part V: Problems/Activities

1.

Directions:
Complete each of the simplified structures below to illustrate the type of passive solar system indicated.

DIRECT GAIN SLOPED WALL

DIRECT GAIN VERTICAL WALL

INDIRECT GAIN TROMBE WALL

INDIRECT GAIN DRUM WALL

| PASSIVE SOLAR HEATING | NAME: | 28-1 |

Directions:
Add solar collectors on the roof, thermal storage with blower in the basement, and connecting ducts to the simplified partial structure below. Show the collectors as 6″ thick and 8′ long, the ducts as 6″ in diameter, and the storage as 4′ × 8′. See Figure 28-13 for design layout.

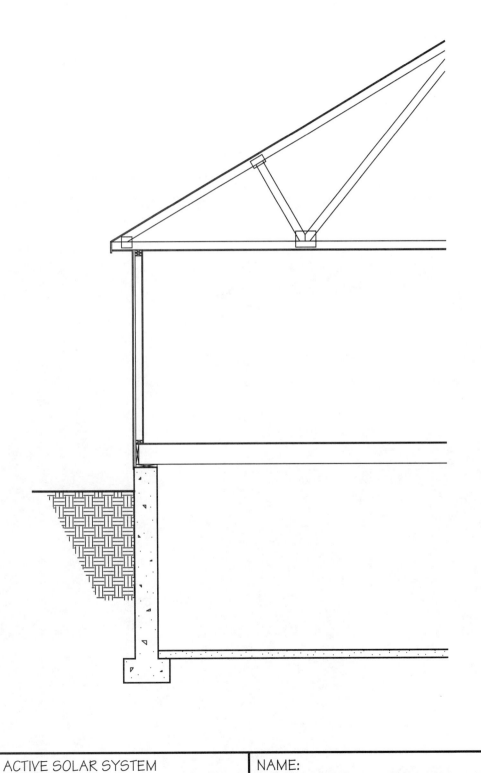

| ACTIVE SOLAR SYSTEM | NAME: | 28-2 |

29 Nontraditional Structures

Text, Pages 565–578

Name _____

Course _____ Date _____ Score _____

Part I: Short Answer/Listing
Provide brief answers to the following questions.

1. List four factors to consider when selecting a site for an earth-sheltered dwelling.

   _____

   _____

2. From which direction do summer breezes originate in northern climates? _____

3. Why are soil type and groundwater considerations so critical when evaluating a site for an earth-sheltered dwelling? _____

   _____

4. Backfill against an earth-sheltered dwelling should be sand or gravel. Why is expansive clay not a viable choice? _____

   _____

5. Name two factors that affect the energy conservation of an earth shelter._____

   _____

6. The two structural systems generally used in earth-sheltered dwellings to support the heavy roof loads are conventional flat roof systems and unconventional systems that use vault and dome shapes. Describe each system.

   Conventional flat roof systems: _____

   _____

   _____

   Vault and dome shapes: _____

   _____

   _____

7. If a suitable site can be found, what are the positive aspects of choosing an earth-sheltered house having a slope design?_____

   _____

   _____

8. What is the approximate reduction in building materials per square foot of usable area for a dome home over conventional construction? _____

9. The true geodesic dome that R. Buckminster Fuller developed uses a series of small triangles. Why have most dome home designers modified Fuller's design? _____

_____

10. A Hexadome uses six panels of triangles to form a raised hexagon. How many hexagons and trapezoids are needed to complete the dome? _____

_____

11. Which piece of equipment is required to place the dome on its foundation? _____

12. What function do riser walls serve in a dome structure? _____

_____

13. Why would a dome structure be a logical house choice in a northern climate where winter temperatures are low and winds are a concern?_____

_____

_____

Part II: Multiple Choice
Select the best answer and write the corresponding letter in the space provided.

1. Orientation to the sun is an important factor in placing earth-sheltered dwellings because:

   1. _____

  A. North-facing orientations are better suited for northern climates.
  B. South-facing orientations are more effective in warm climates.
  C. Solar energy may be used to heat the interior space.
  D. All of the above.

2. Site selection for an earth-sheltered dwelling is very important. Sites that are _____ permit greater design possibilities.

   2. _____

  A. sloping
  B. flat
  C. Both A and B.
  D. None of the above.

3. Soil characteristics affecting the design of the structure include:

   3. _____

  A. Soil color and depth of the topsoil.
  B. Bearing capacity and tendency to expand when wet.
  C. All of the above.
  D. None of the above.

4. Soils that have the optimum bearing capacity and should be used under the foundation of an earth-sheltered dwelling are:

   A. Fine grained soils.
   B. Rock 2″ to 3″ in diameter.
   C. Expansive clay.
   D. Compacted sand or gravel.

4. _____

5. Generally, an earth-sheltered structure that will conserve the greatest amount of energy:

   A. Has a small surface area exposed.
   B. Has a large surface area exposed.
   C. Is long across the front and narrow on the sides.
   D. Has two levels.

5. _____

6. The advantage(s) of choosing an earth-sheltered dwelling over a conventional dwelling is(are):

   A. A longer life span.
   B. Less maintenance.
   C. Lower energy needs.
   D. All of the above.

6. _____

7. The living areas are located around a central courtyard in the atrium design. This design is:

   A. Better suited for warm climates.
   B. Convenient for efficient traffic circulation in cold climates.
   C. A compact plan.
   D. Suitable for south-facing windows.

7. _____

8. An advantage of selecting an earth-sheltered house is:

   A. Most contractors are generally quite knowledge-able about their construction requirements.
   B. Their high resistance to fire damage.
   C. They are adaptable to any neighborhood setting.
   D. Code requirements present no problems.

8. _____

9. The geodesic dome is based on which shape?

   A. Triangle.
   B. Rectangle.
   C. Circle.
   D. Trapezoid.

9. _____

10. The dome provides an open interior space because:

   A. Interior walls or beams would interfere with the floor plan.
   B. The structure of the dome is self supporting.
   C. Mr. Fuller did not like interior walls.
   D. The ceilings are too high for support walls.

10. _____

11. Two basic domes have evolved from the original geodesic dome. Both use triangles to form:

   A. Pentagons, trapezoids, and rectangles.
   B. Hexagons, pentagons, and rectangles.
   C. Hexagons, pentagons, and trapezoids.
   D. All of the above.

11. _____

12. Cutting the proper _____ is critical for the pieces to join together properly in a dome structure.

   A. circles
   B. angles
   C. Both A and B.
   D. None of the above.

12. _____

13. The foundation for a dome can be a:

   A. Basement.
   B. Crawl space.
   C. Slab foundation.
   D. All of the above.

13. _____

14. Riser walls have _____ walls on each side to completely enclose the structure.

   A. wing
   B. side
   C. top
   D. bottom

14. _____

Part III: Completion
Complete each sentence with the proper response. Place your answer on the space provided.

1. An earth-sheltered dwelling built in Michigan will be most efficient if windows and doors are placed on the _____ side of the structure to prevent heat loss from the cold winter winds.

1. _____

2. To provide shade in warm seasons and permit sun penetration in cool seasons, plant _____ trees, which lose their leaves in the autumn.

2. _____

3. Soil on the roof of an earth-sheltered structure should be _____ grained to support vegetation and prevent frost heave.

3. _____

4. Sites with _____ drainage provide the best conditions to support an earth-sheltered home.

4. _____

5. Energy conservation is usually high when a _____ area of the structure has an earth cover.

5. _____

6. The _____ design of an earth-sheltered dwelling has windows and doors on one side of the dwelling.

6. _____

7. The _____ design of an earth-sheltered dwelling permits windows and doors at certain points around the structure.

7. _____

8. The original geodesic dome was developed by _____.

8. _____

9. Common exterior materials for dome structures include _____ shingles and cedar shakes.

9. _____

10. Domes may be constructed similar to conventional homes—the panels can be purchased complete and ready to bolt together, _____ at the factory and shipped as individual pieces, or built completely on site from standard lumber and plywood.

10. _____

Directions:
Draw a simplified section view of a single-level residential structure of the slope design for the site indicated below by the dotted line. (See Figure 29-8 in the text.) The plan should incorporate the following: 8' ceiling, 24' depth (front to back), 2' of soil on top of a 1' thick ceiling, glass wall on south side, and 4' bubble-type skylight near the rear of the home. Scale is 1/8" = 1'-0".

| EARTH-SHELTERED HOME | NAME: | 29-1 |

Directions:
Study the topographical drawing of the site below and show the placement of a 24' × 60' earth-sheltered home of the slope design. The location should take into consideration the direction of the sun for maximum heating, direction of winter winds and summer breezes, patterns of water runoff, and groundwater conditions. The scale of the drawing is 1/16" = 1'-0".

Winter wind from NW, summer breezes from SE, and sun from S.

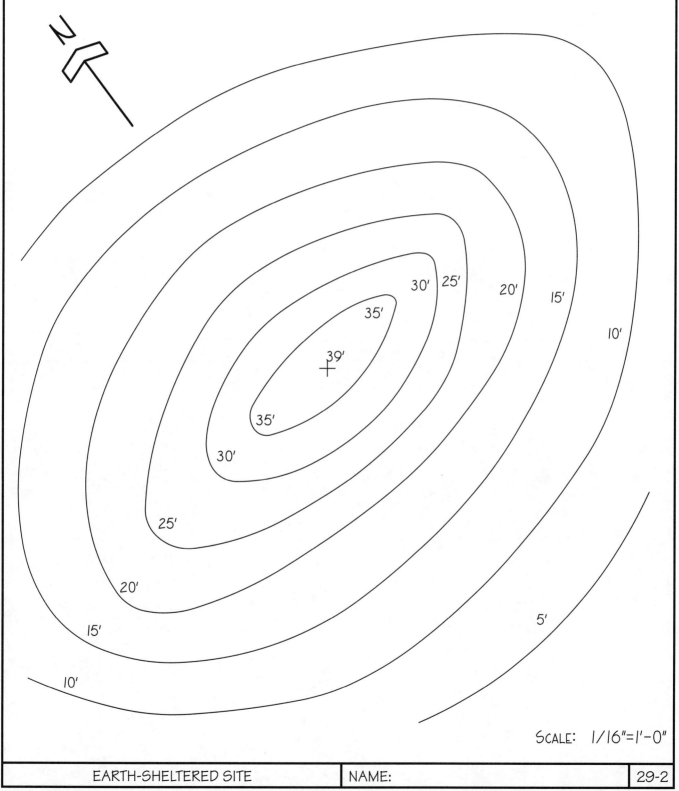

SCALE: 1/16"=1'-0"

| EARTH-SHELTERED SITE | NAME: | 29-2 |

Directions:

Scale the manufacturer's drawings of the 45' diameter dome home below and draw the basic shape (upper and lower levels) at a scale of 1/4" = 1'-0" on C-size paper. Modify the interior space to suit yourself, but in keeping with good design principles. Remember, headroom is reduced near the exterior walls in most locations on the upper level.

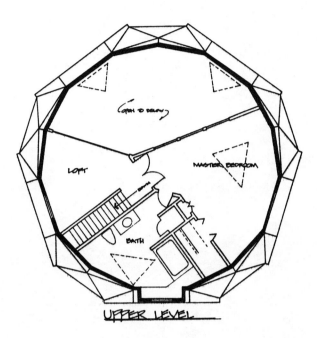

UPPER LEVEL

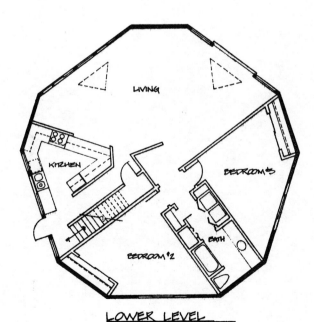

LOWER LEVEL

Directions:
Using the dimensions below, build a 32' diameter dome model at 1/2" or 1" scale. Riser walls should be approximately 2' high. Use foam board, heavy illustration board, or thin wood paneling to form each module. Accuracy is very important!

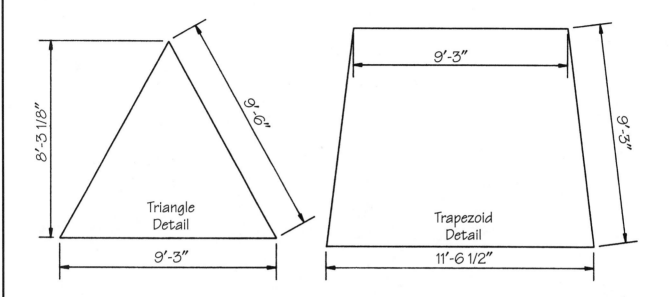

Triangle
Detail

8'-3 1/8"

9'-6"

9'-3"

Trapezoid
Detail

9'-3"

9'-3"

11'-6 1/2"

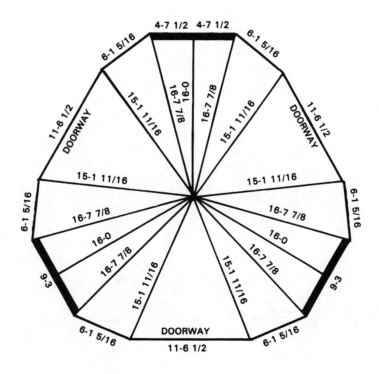

4-7 1/2   4-7 1/2

6-1 5/16   6-1 5/16

16-0

16-7 7/8   16-7 7/8

15-1 11/16   15-1 11/16

11-6 1/2
DOORWAY   DOORWAY
11-6 1/2

15-1 11/16   15-1 11/16

6-1 5/16   6-1 5/16

16-7 7/8   16-7 7/8

16-0   16-0

16-7 7/8   16-7 7/8

9-3   9-3

15-1 11/16   15-1 11/16

6-1 5/16   6-1 5/16

DOORWAY

11-6 1/2

New Products and Methods of Construction

Text, Pages 579–596

Name _____

Course _____ Date _____ Score _____

Part I: Short Answer/Listing
Provide brief answers to the following questions.

1. Where is the rigid foam insulation placed in a frost-protected shallow foundation?_____

   _____

   _____

2. Name two categories of alternatives to pressure-treated deck material. _____

   _____

   _____

3. What is another name for exterior insulation finish systems (EIFS)? _____

   _____

4. Name the two generic types of EIFS. _____

   _____

5. What size are Hebel blocks? How much do they weigh? _____

   _____

6. What are the typical thicknesses of structural foam sandwich panels? _____

   _____

7. What are two other names for "Philippine mahogany?" _____

   _____

8. What does the acronym "HDPE" stand for? _____

   _____

9. Name two disadvantages of weather-resistant deck materials. _____

   _____

   _____

10. Name four states where there is a high probability of termite infestation. _____

    _____

    _____

11. Describe the construction of a structural foam sandwich panel. _____

_____

_____

_____

12. What is the driving force behind the development of new concrete wall systems? _____

_____

13. Describe the two main categories of insulated concrete wall forms._____

_____

_____

_____

_____

14. What are three advantages of the Therma-Lock™ block system? _____

_____

_____

_____

_____

Part II: Multiple Choice

Select the best answer and write the corresponding letter in the space provided.

1. Which of the following is *not* a synthetic decking product?

   A. Trex®
   B. Perma-Poly™
   C. TimberTech®
   D. Integra™

1. _____

2. Which of the following is a characteristic of EIFS PB systems?

   A. The flexibility reduces the need for numerous control joints.
   B. They can tolerate prolonged wetting.
   C. They are usually thicker than 1/4".
   D. They are called "hard-coat" systems.

2. _____

3. Which of the following is *not* an advantage provided by structural foam sandwich panels?

   A. Durability over time.
   B. Speed of erection.
   C. Less moisture migration.
   D. Superior energy performance.

3. _____

Name _____

4. Which of the following products may be described as interlocking blocks of plastic foam insulation that are stackable and whose hollow cores are filled with concrete?

4. _____

    A. Lite-Form™
    B. Thermomass™
    C. SmartBlock™
    D. Plasti-Fab Enermizer Building Systems™

5. What is the standard size of a welded-wire sandwich panel?

5. _____

    A. 2′ × 4′
    B. 4′ × 4′
    C. 4′ × 8′
    D. 4′ × 16′

Part III: Completion
Complete each sentence with the proper response. Place your answer on the space provided.

1. OSB stands for _____.

1. _____

2. CMU stands for _____.

2. _____

3. The maximum length of welded-wire sandwich panels is _____ feet.

3. _____

4. What softwood is generally used for pressure-treated lumber?

4. _____

Part IV: Problems/Activities

1.

Directions:
Design a 300 square foot to 400 square foot rear deck for the house below. Show a plan view of the deck with dimensions and details necessary for construction. Specify one of the weather-resistant decking materials discussed in the text. Assume the grade to be 24" below the floor level of the house with a slope of 1:12 away from the house.

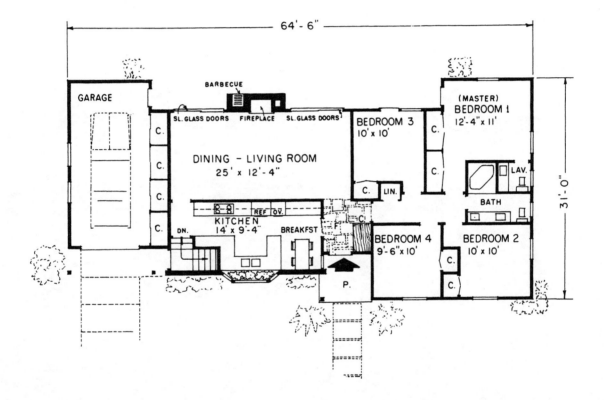

| NEW DECK MATERIALS | NAME: | 30-1 |

Modular Applications
31

Text, Pages 597–605

Name _____

Course _____ Date _____ Score _____

Part I: Completion
Complete each sentence with the proper response. Place your answer on the space provided.

1. Residential structures have traditionally been built by fastening together thousands of small pieces, such as boards, bricks, etc., on the job site. This is referred to as _____.

1. _____

2. Standard-size building materials are required in _____ construction.

2. _____

3. Widths ranging from 16" to 196" in multiples of _____ are often common for modular panel components.

3. _____

4. An arrowhead terminator indicates that the dimension ends on the grid line while a _____ terminator indicates that the dimension ends off the grid line.

4. _____

5. Modular _____ are building parts that have been preassembled either in a plant or on-site.

5. _____

6. The term _____ refers to houses built in a factory.

6. _____

Part II: Short Answer/Listing
Provide brief answers to the following questions.

1. What are two benefits gained by using modular sizes and mass production in house construction? _____

_____

2. Modular construction is based on the standard module, which is a 4" cube. Name the other two modules and their sizes typically found in modular construction. _____

_____

3. For drawing and dimensioning modular houses, what should a designer or drafter use to help with layout? _____

4. What are modular components? _____

_____

5. List three advantages of prefabricated panels (panelized construction). _____

_____

_____

6. Why is the quality of many factory-built homes better than traditional construction?

_____

_____

Part III: Multiple Choice
Select the best answer and write the corresponding letter in the space provided.

1. Houses that are built in the factory to the specifications of prospective owners are referred to as:

   A. Custom homes.
   B. Mobile homes.
   C. Industrialized housing.
   D. All of the above.

   1. _____

2. Studs and joists are placed 16"OC and 24"OC to coincide with _____ modules.

   A. standard
   B. minor
   C. major
   D. All of the above.

   2. _____

3. When drawing a modular floor plan, details of the structure should begin and end:

   A. On grid lines.
   B. Above grid lines.
   C. Below grid lines.
   D. None of the above.

   3. _____

4. Floor panels, roof panels, wall sections, or roof trusses are all examples of:

   A. Partitions.
   B. Modular components.
   C. Stock lumber.
   D. All of the above.

   4. _____

5. In factory-built houses:

   A. The quality is generally not as good as in traditional construction.
   B. The quality of lumber is unimportant.
   C. Jigs and fixtures are used to cut and fit parts together.
   D. None of the above.

   5. _____

6. A characteristic of factory-built houses is:

   A. The modules are usually complete with plumbing, wiring, finished floors, and doors.
   B. They require a special foundation.
   C. Little versatility of modules is possible.
   D. All of the above.

   6. _____

Part IV: Problems/Activities

1.

Directions:
Using the modular grid below, draw the plan view wall framing plan for a 10'-0" × 12'-0" frame storage building with siding. Be sure to apply the modular concepts presented in the text. Provide an access door at least 36" wide and two windows in your design. The scale is 1/2" = 1'-0".

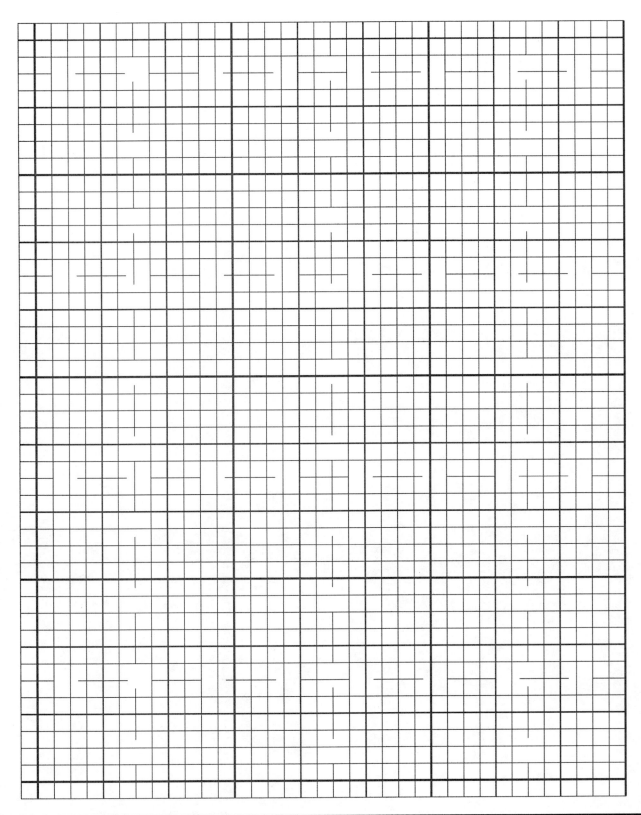

| MODULAR CONSTRUCTION | NAME: | 31-1 |

Perspective Drawings

32

Text, Pages 607–635

Name _____

Course _____ Date _____ Score _____

Part I: Matching
Match the correct term with its description listed below. Place the corresponding letter on the space provided.

A. Ground line
B. Horizon line
C. Perspective
D. Perspective grid
E. Picture plane

F. Rendering
G. Station point
H. Three-point perspective
I. True length line
J. Vanishing points

1. A type of pictorial drawing that gives a realistic view of the object.

2. Also called an oblique perspective.

3. Represents a horizontal plane called the ground plane.

4. The place where the ground and sky meet.

5. A vertical plane on which the perspective is drawn.

6. The location of the observer's eye.

7. A line used to project heights onto a perspective drawing.

8. Always located on the horizon line.

9. Adding shading or coloring to a drawing.

10. Saves time and space in drawing a large perspective.

1. _____

2. _____

3. _____

4. _____

5. _____

6. _____

7. _____

8. _____

9. _____

10. _____

Part II: Short Answer/Listing
Provide brief answers to the following questions.

1. Name the three types of perspectives and indicate a typical use for each type. _____

_____

_____

_____

2. List the three parts in a perspective layout. _____

_____

_____

3. In how many views is the station point located when creating a one-point perspective? ____

_____

4. When drawing a two-point perspective, what are the two most common angles between the sides of the object and the picture plane? _____

_____

5. List two factors that determine the height of the horizon line. _____

_____

6. In a two-point perspective, what is the angular relationship between the picture plane, ground line, and horizon line? _____

7. Explain how the left and right vanishing points are determined in a two-point perspective.

_____

_____

_____

_____

_____

_____

8. Explain how you would draw a chair with soft curves in perspective. _____

_____

_____

Part III: Multiple Choice
Select the best answer and write the corresponding letter in the space provided.

1. One-point perspectives are _____ perspectives.   1. _____

   A. oblique
   B. angular
   C. parallel
   D. All of the above.

2. When an object is placed behind the picture plane and   2. _____
the station point is above the ground line:

   A. It must touch the ground line in the perspective of the object.
   B. The perspective of the object will be above the ground line.
   C. The object will extend below the ground line.
   D. None of the above.

Name _____

3. Two-point perspectives are good communicators   3. _____
because:

   A. They generate a photo-like drawing that is very
      accurate in detail.
   B. The objects are drawn true to size.
   C. They are quite simple to draw.
   D. None of the above.

4. Generally, the station point is placed so that it forms a   4. _____
cone of vision between _____.

   A. 15° and 30°
   B. 15° and 22-1/2°
   C. 30° and 45°
   D. All of the above.

5. The most frequently used method for drawing one-   5. _____
and two-point perspectives is the:

   A. Common method.
   B. Office method.
   C. Both A and B.
   D. None of the above.

6. The elevation should be placed on the _____ at the   6. _____
extreme right or left in a two-point perspective.

   A. picture plane
   B. ground line
   C. horizon line
   D. None of the above.

Part IV: Completion
Complete each sentence with the proper response. Place your answer on the space provided.

1. In perspectives, the _____ is the location of the   1. _____
observer's eye.

2. Any part of the object that is in front of the picture   2. _____
plane will appear _____ than the correct scale.

3. If the _____ is placed too close to the picture plane, the   3. _____
drawing will be unrealistic and distorted.

4. To obtain a "bird's eye view" of the object, locate the   4. _____
station point or horizon line approximately _____
above the ground line.

5. When drawing a large two-point perspective, draw the   5. _____
_____ and elevation on separate sheets of paper.

6. The height of features that are not located on the principal sides of the object, such as roof ridges, overhangs, and chimneys, may be quickly determined by establishing a new _____ line.

7. The vanishing point may not be located in a _____-point perspective.

8. Circular or oval objects may be drawn by locating several _____ on the surface to be drawn and then connecting them together.

9. When drawing CADD perspectives, one of the biggest advantages of a(n) _____ model is that the object can be viewed from any angle.

10. In addition to generating perspectives, many CADD software with 3D capabilities can shade or color the drawing through a process called _____.

6. _____

7. _____

8. _____

9. _____

10. _____

Part V: Problems/Activities

1.

Directions:
Label each of the parts indicated on the two-point perspective layout below.

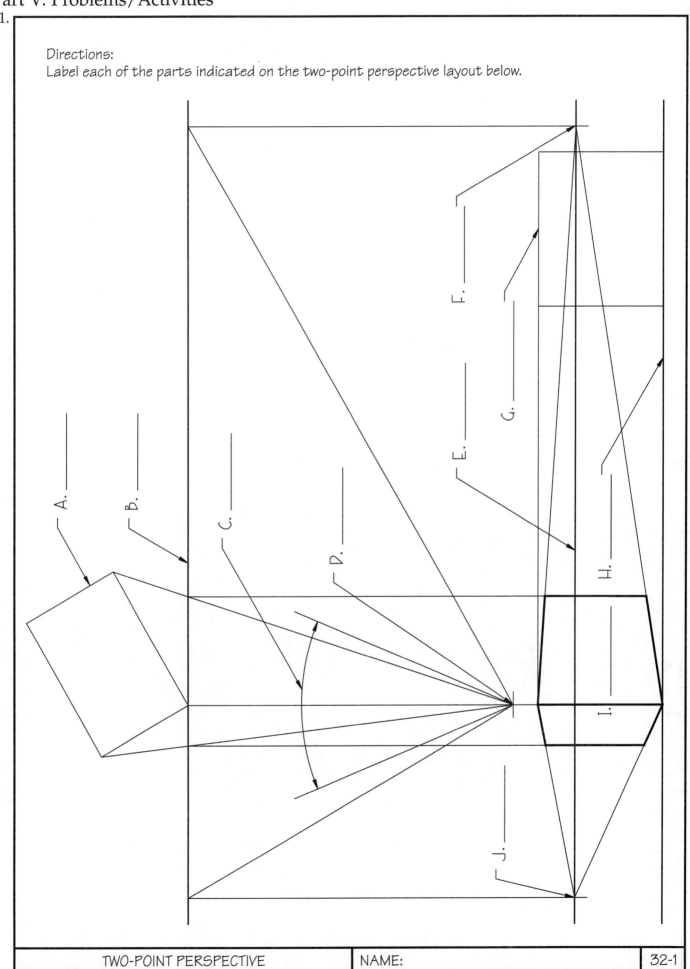

A. _____

B. _____

C. _____

D. _____

E. _____

F. _____

G. _____

H. _____

I. _____

J. _____

TWO-POINT PERSPECTIVE   NAME: _____   32-1

Chapter 32 Perspective Drawings   **345**

2.

Directions:
Draw a two-point perspective of the object using the setup provided. Show all construction lines, but use wider visible object lines. Omit hidden lines from the pictorial.

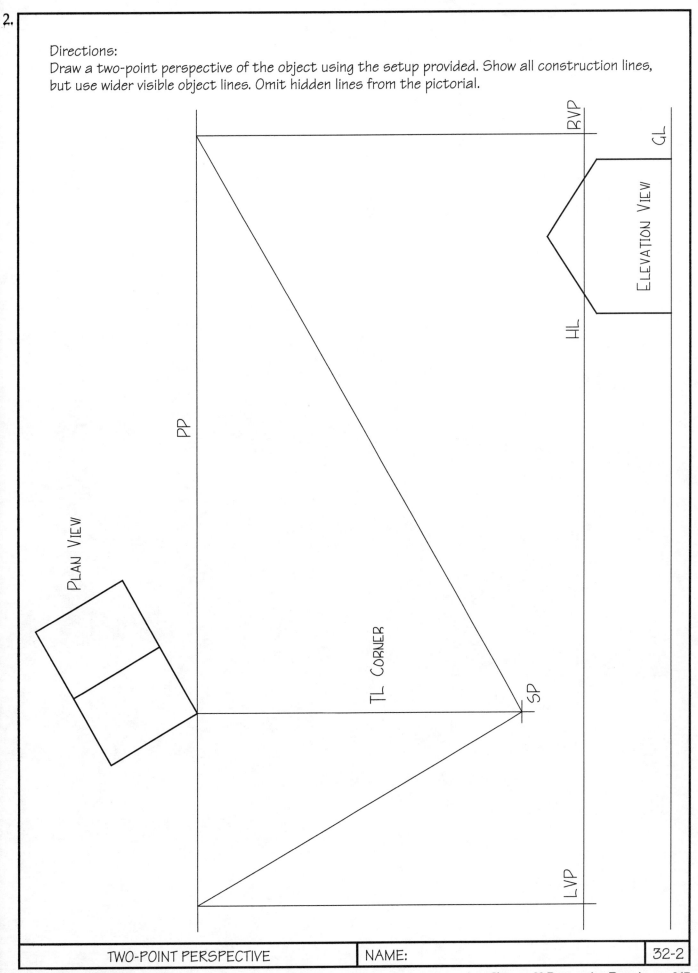

RVP

GL

ELEVATION VIEW

HL

PP

PLAN VIEW

TL CORNER

SP

LVP

TWO-POINT PERSPECTIVE | NAME: | 32-2

3.

Directions:
Draw a two-point perspective of the object as indicated. Show all construction lines, but use wider visible object lines. Omit hidden lines in the pictorial.

RVP

GL

HL

PP

SP

LVP

| TWO-POINT PERSPECTIVE | NAME: | 32-3 |

4. **Two-point perspective.** Using the elevation and floor plan/foundation plan of the garage in Figure 9-42 of the text, set up a two-point perspective layout on a C-size sheet. Construct the perspective from an appropriate position. Follow the procedure described in the text. The solution will be evaluated on accuracy as well as the quality of the view.

5.

Directions:
Complete the one-point perspective drawing below using the procedure described in the text.
Show your construction using light construction lines. Darken the visible object lines.

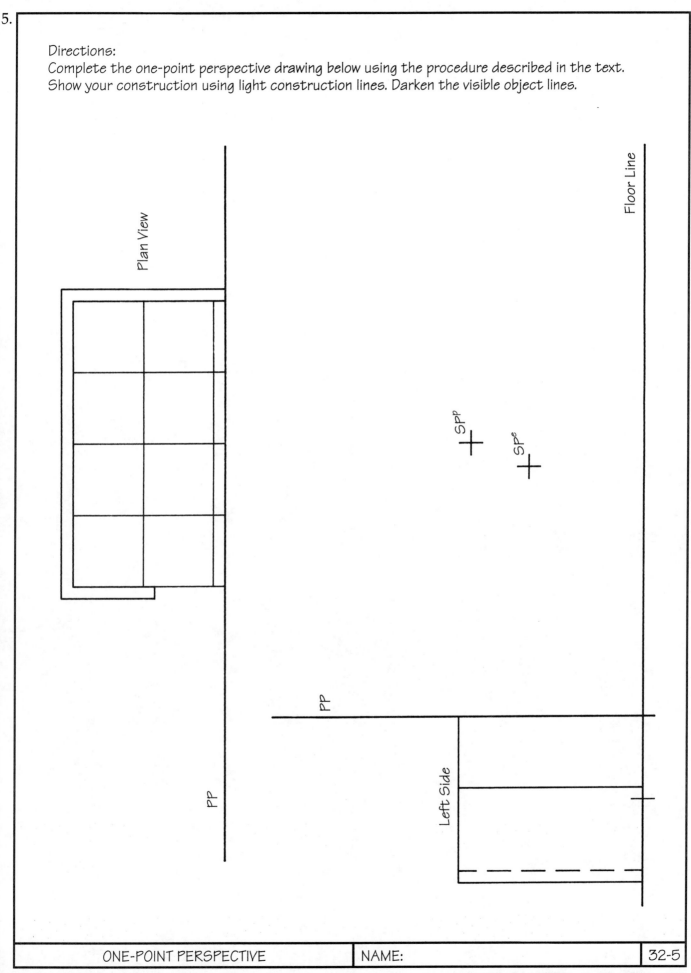

Plan View

PP

Floor Line

SP^P

SP^e

PP

Left Side

6.

Directions:
Draw a one-point perspective of the room, table, and rug indicated below. Show construction lines as very light lines. Darken visible object lines and omit hidden lines.

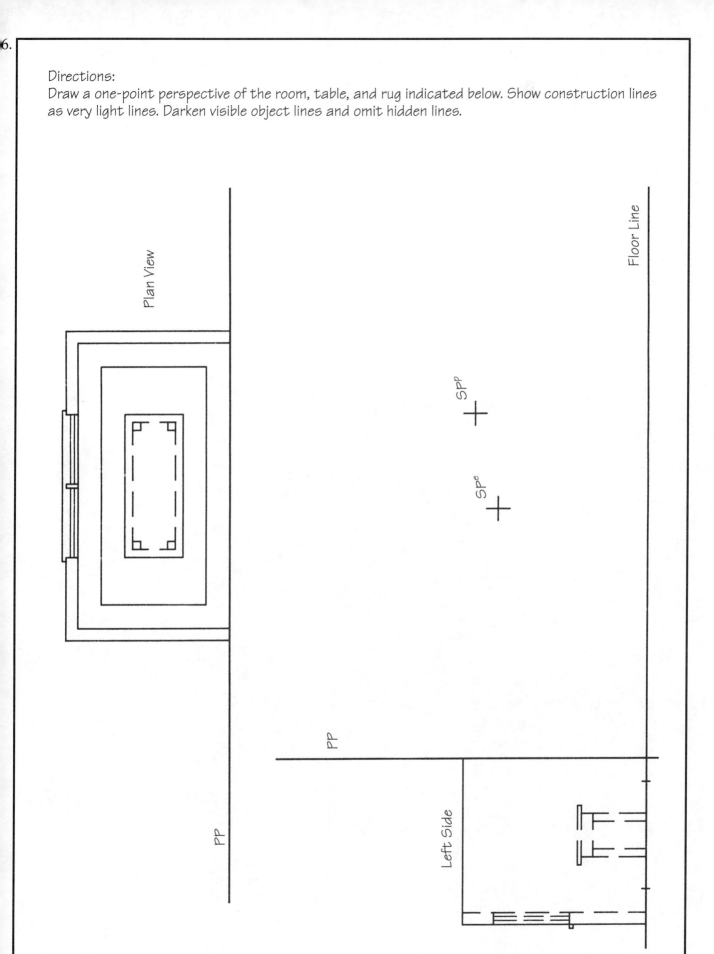

Plan View

PP

Floor Line

SP^p

SP^e

PP

Left Side

7.

Directions:
Draw a one-point perspective of the room and contents (simplified furniture pieces) below. Show construction lines as very light lines. Darken visible object lines and omit hidden lines.

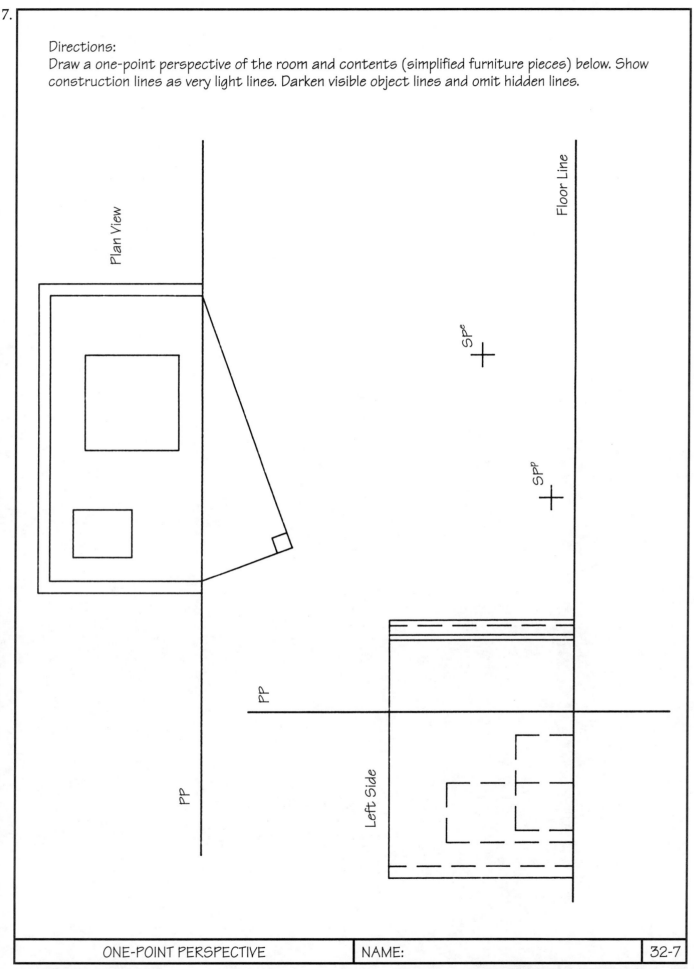

Plan View

Floor Line

SP^e

SP^p

PP

PP

Left Side

8. **One-point perspective.** Using the kitchen plan that you designed for Suggested Activity #3 in Chapter 9 of the text, set up a one-point perspective layout on C-size paper. Draw a perspective that accurately communicates the features of your design. Follow the procedure described in the text. The evaluation will consider the communication of the drawing as well as accuracy of your construction.

33 Presentation Drawings

Text, Pages 637–660

Name _____

Course _____ Date _____ Score _____

Part I: Short Answer/Listing
Provide brief answers to the following questions.

1. Why are presentation drawings made in addition to construction drawings? _____

   _____

   _____

2. Name four types of presentation drawings or plans commonly used to represent a structure.

   _____

   _____

3. Briefly describe how appliqué rendering is accomplished. _____

   _____

   _____

4. When creating a computer-generated rendering, what determines the amount of lighting needed on a given surface? _____

   _____

Part II: Multiple Choice
Select the best answer and write the corresponding letter in the space provided.

1. Of the following types of renderings, which is probably   1. _____
   the easiest to complete?

   A. Watercolor
   B. Pencil
   C. Airbrush
   D. Ink

2. Which type of rendering is best suited for reproduction?   2. _____

   A. Pencil
   B. Ink
   C. Felt-tipped pen
   D. Tempera

3. _____ renderings require a great deal of practice to do successfully and are frequently produced by professional illustrators.

   A. Felt-tipped pen
   B. Appliqué
   C. Colored pencil
   D. Airbrush

3. _____

4. Which type of rendering consists of white lines on a black background?

   A. Felt-tipped pen
   B. Appliqué
   C. Scratchboard
   D. Tempera

4. _____

5. Triangle lighting involves placing a fill light _____.

   A. in front of the scene
   B. toward the rear of the scene
   C. to bring the object out of the background
   D. to remove shadows

5. _____

Part III: Completion
Complete each sentence with the proper response. Place your answer on the space provided.

1. _____ renderings use a water-soluble paint and are frequently used for monotone renderings.

1. _____

2. A _____ is a special white illustration board with a black coating.

2. _____

3. Features such as people, trees, and cars provide a more realistic setting for a presentation drawing and are referred to as _____.

3. _____

4. A presentation _____ plan shows the relationship between the site and structure and provides a bird's eye view of the layout.

4. _____

5. The _____ light provides most of the illumination in triangle lighting.

5. _____

6. To determine the areas of an object that should be shaded, the angle of the sun or _____ must first be established.

6. _____

7. A _____ shows an animated view of how a building would appear to a person actually walking through it.

7. _____

8. An animation frame on which an important action takes place is called a _____.

8. _____

Part IV: Problems/Activities

1.

Directions:
Make a pencil rendering of the scene shown below. Use a piece of tracing vellum over the photo to produce the rendering. Use texture to add realism to the drawing.

| PENCIL RENDERING | NAME: | 33-1 |

2.

Directions:
Make an ink rendering of the cast concrete structure below. Use a piece of tracing vellum over the photo to produce the drawing. Add texture to the drawing to produce a realistic appearance.

| INK RENDERING | NAME: | 33-2 |

3. **Rendering.** Use the front elevation that you drew for Problem 20-3 as the subject for this activity. Render it on paper or illustration board as a colored pencil, watercolor, tempera, or felt-tipped pen rendering. This assignment will be evaluated based on realism and accuracy.

4.

Directions:
Using the floor plan and hand-rendered perspective below as a guide, develop a rendered 3D perspective model of this residence on your CADD system. Be sure to maintain the relative proportions of the structure. Strive for realism.

Sater Design Collections, Inc.

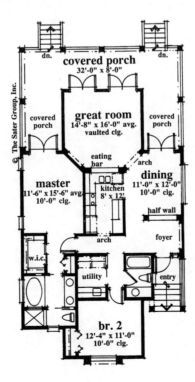

Architectural Models

34

Text, Pages 661–673

Name _____

Course _____ Date _____ Score _____

Part I: Multiple Choice
Select the best answer and write the corresponding letter in the space provided.

1. A _____ model shows only the exterior shape of the building and is not hollow.

   A. small scale solid
   B. structural
   C. presentation
   D. All of the above.

   1. _____

2. The scale of structural models is usually _____.

   A. 1/4″ = 1′-0″ or 1/2″ = 1′-0″
   B. 1″ = 1′-0″ or 2″ = 1′-0″
   C. 1/2″ = 1′-0″ or 1″ = 1′-0″
   D. None of the above.

   2. _____

3. Foam board is often used in building model structures because:

   A. It will not scratch or break easily.
   B. It can be finished to resemble various exterior building materials.
   C. Both A and B.
   D. None of the above.

   3. _____

4. Before gluing the exterior walls of a presentation model, compare each wall with the _____ to ensure accuracy.

   A. floor plan
   B. foundation plan
   C. site plan
   D. All of the above.

   4. _____

5. Interior walls of presentation models are typically _____ thick balsa.

   A. 1/16″
   B. 1/8″
   C. 1/4″
   D. None of the above.

   5. _____

6. _____ or _____ paint colors are often used on interior walls of a model.

    A. Transparent; light
    B. Dark; light
    C. White; black
    D. White; soft pastel

6. _____

Part II: Completion

Complete each sentence with the proper response. Place your answer on the space provided.

1. The scale of small scale solid models may range from $1/32'' = 1'\text{-}0''$ to _____.

1. _____

2. An architect will most likely choose a(n) _____ model to show the most realistic appearance of a residential structure.

2. _____

3. A model-building material that is easy to work with, does not easily warp, lends itself to different kinds of finishes, and strong is _____.

3. _____

4. A good-size base for an average residence is $30'' \times 30''$ or _____.

4. _____

5. Wall corners may be mitered or butt jointed; _____ is usually neater.

5. _____

6. A material that is useful for windows in models is $1/16''$ thick _____.

6. _____

7. The most satisfactory results are usually obtained by assembling the roof on the _____.

7. _____

8. Using $1/4''$ balsa for roof sheathing will approximately duplicate the scaled thickness of the rafters and _____ on a house.

8. _____

9. The plants may be purchased or fabricated from a _____ and/or _____.

9. _____
_____

Part III: Short Answer/Listing

Provide brief answers to the following questions.

1. Name the three types of models commonly used to represent structures. _____

_____

_____

2. If you were a building contractor and decided to use a model to illustrate an innovative building technique, which type of model would be best? _____

_____

3. What scale is commonly used for presentation models? _____

Name _____

4. List three materials that can be used to build up elevated areas to represent a rolling terrain.

_____

5. Name the two plans or drawings generally required to build a model._____

_____

6. How thick should the exterior walls of a presentation model be for a residential structure with frame walls if balsa is used?_____

_____

7. How can flashing be represented on a presentation model? _____

_____

8. How can mortar joints be given an authentic appearance on an architectural model? _____

_____

9. What material can be used to represent roofing materials? _____

Part IV: Problems/Activities

1. **Architectural Model.** Using the garden house from Problems/Activities 12-1 and 20-3 in this workbook, construct a presentation model of the structure at 1/4" = 1'-0" scale. Heavy illustration board, 1/8" plywood, balsa wood, or foam board can be used to construct the roof and walls. Sandpaper strips can be used to represent asphalt shingles. Supplies are generally available at a local hobby shop. Paint or stain the walls for realism. Mount the completed model on a base for protection and handling. Study the text for procedures and useful hints.

2. **Structural Model.** Construct a structural model of the garden house from Problems/Activities 12-1 and 20-3 in this workbook at a scale of 1" = 1'-0". The purpose of this model is to show the actual construction. Therefore, leave sections of the framing members exposed to view. Balsa or poplar wood is generally used for framing members and balsa sheets are recommended for panel products. Mount the completed model on a 1/4" plywood base.

3. **Ranch House Model.** Construct a presentation model at 1/4" = 1'-0" of the ranch style home you designed for Problems/Activities 18-3 and 20-4 in this workbook. Your instructor will provide specific instructions for this assignment.

Material and Tradework Specifications

Text, Pages 675–684

Name _____

Course _____ Date _____ Score _____

Part I: Short Answer/Listing
Provide brief answers to the following questions.

1. Which document lists the types of materials, fixtures, and other physical items? _____
_____

2. Along with working drawings, what becomes part of the total contract between the builder and owner? _____
_____

3. What can the client do to assure a certain level of quality workmanship in the house?
_____
_____

4. Where may specification forms be obtained? _____
_____
_____

5. Who is usually responsible for liability during the construction process?_____

Part II: Completion
Complete each sentence with the proper response. Place your answer on the space provided.

1. The architect and customer usually develop a "_____ outline" together.

1. _____

2. Generally, the _____ should have the greatest input on materials, while the _____ will have more input on interior finishing, appliances, and fixtures.

2. _____
_____

3. The required _____ operations—excavation, masonry, carpentry, millwork, plumbing, electrical, and insulation—should be described in the specifications.

3. _____

4. Cash allowances are generally set up for items such as lighting fixtures. The _____ is usually responsible for any money spent above the allowance.

4. _____

5. A description of the materials to be used should include sizes, quality, _____ names, style, and specification numbers.

5. _____

Part III: Problems/Activities

1. **Contract Specifications.** Download the *Description of Materials* form from the Department of Veterans Affairs web site or use the form shown in the text. Fill out the form as completely as possible for the ranch home you designed in previous assignments in this workbook or use a set of working drawings provided by your instructor. Plan the specifications as though you will be the owner. Select items from current catalogs and manufacturers' literature.

Estimating Building Cost

36

Text, Pages 685–693

Name _____

Course _____ Date _____ Score _____

Part I: Completion
Complete each sentence with the proper response. Place your answer on the space provided.

1. A systematic attempt to arrive at the cost of materials, labor, and other services needed to build a house is _____.

   1. _____

2. Since building costs per square foot vary from one section of the country to another, check with local _____ to determine the correct cost for your area.

   2. _____

3. In the square foot method, the cost is based on _____, while in the cubic foot method, the cost is based on volume.

   3. _____

4. Two documents should be studied very carefully for use as the basis for estimating the cost of a structure. These are the construction drawings and _____.

   4. _____

5. To estimate the cost of a house using the cubic foot method, multiply the area by the _____.

   5. _____

Part II: Short Answer/Listing
Provide brief answers to the following questions.

1. In general, how expensive are ranch-style homes in comparison to two-story homes providing you are estimating the same living area? _____

   _____

2. To find the area of a house in square feet, multiply the length by the width. Should wall thickness be included?_____

3. What are two items, besides materials and labor, that should be included in the cost of building a house?_____

   _____

4. Describe another way to estimate the cost of a home that is probably more accurate than the square foot method or cubic foot method._____

   _____

   _____

   _____

5. What is the relationship between the headings on a materials list and the construction sequence?_____

_____

6. The cost of permits should be included when estimating the cost of building a house. List the permits that may be needed. _____

_____

_____

Part III: Multiple Choice

Select the best answer and write the corresponding letter in the space provided.

1. Porches, garages, and basements are figured at _____ the cost per square foot of the living area.

    A. one-eighth
    B. one-fourth
    C. one-half
    D. three-fourths

1. _____

2. Using the square foot method, how much is the building cost for a 24' × 60' house and a 20' × 20' detached garage if the cost per square foot is $100?

    A. $144,000
    B. $164,000
    C. $184,000
    D. $204,000

2. _____

3. What is the total volume of a 20' × 20' garage with standard height walls if the garage attic has a rise of 3'?

    A. 3,200 cubic feet
    B. 3,400 cubic feet
    C. 3,600 cubic feet
    D. 3,800 cubic feet

3. _____

4. Labor costs usually range from _____ of the total cost of the house.

    A. 30% to 50%
    B. 40% to 60%
    C. 50% to 70%
    D. 60% to 80%

4. _____

1.

Directions:

Prepare a materials list for the garden house used in Problems 12-1 and 20-3 or another building provided by your instructor. Use the following headings in the materials list: General Information, Masonry, Carpenter's Lumber List, Windows and Screens, Doors and Trim, Cabinets and Miscellaneous Millwork, Insulation, Weatherstripping and Caulking, Plastering or Drywall, Finish Flooring, Painting and Finishing, Hardware, Finish Hardware, Sheet Metal Work, Floor Finishing Material, Wall Finishing Material, Roofing, Plumbing, Electrical Wiring, Telephone Wiring, and Heating. Follow the complete list in the text.

Materials List

MATERIALS LIST	NAME:	36-1

| MATERIALS LIST | NAME: | 36-1 |

MATERIALS LIST   NAME: 36-1

| MATERIALS LIST | NAME: | 36-1 |

37 Architectural Remodeling, Renovation, and Preservation

Text, Pages 695–713

Name _____

Course _____ Date _____ Score _____

Part I: Matching
Match the correct term with its description listed below. Place the corresponding letter on the space provided.

A. Adaptive reuse E. Historic preservation
B. Attic F. Moisture barrier
C. Dehumidifying system G. Remodeling
D. Dormer H. Restoration

1. The process of changing the function of a building. 1. _____

2. Returning a building to its original condition while maintaining traditional styles, materials, and in some cases furnishings. 2. _____

3. Allow in natural light and increase the amount of usable space in an attic by adding headroom. 3. _____

4. The space between the ceiling and the roof. 4. _____

5. Changing an existing space into a new form. 5. _____

6. Infers that a structure is returned to its original condition. 6. _____

7. Removes moisture vapor from the air to reduce the relative humidity in the space. 7. _____

8. A membrane that retards the flow of moisture vapor and reduces condensation. 8. _____

Part II: Completion
Complete each sentence with the proper response. Place your answer on the space provided.

1. The least complex types of remodeling involve making changes in rooms already used or changing a(n) _____ space so it can be used as a living area. 1. _____

2. The _____ is usually the most expensive room to remodel. 2. _____

3. Like kitchens, _____ are often remodeled to update old fixtures.

3. _____

4. Generally, rooms that do not have major _____ can be changed dramatically with relatively minor remodeling projects.

4. _____

5. An unfinished _____ is frequently remodeled to be used as a family room, recreation room, hobby area, or workshop.

5. _____

6. Remodeled basement areas are often _____, so vapor barriers and a dehumidifying system should be added for comfort.

6. _____

7. Once a basement is converted into a living area, a direct exit to the _____ may be required by the code.

7. _____

8. Adequate headroom of at least _____ should be allowed between the floor and finished ceiling in a remodeled attic.

8. _____

9. Dormers allow natural light and increase the amount of usable space in a(n) _____ by adding headroom.

9. _____

10. Adding on to a home usually involves the removal of all or part of an _____ wall.

10. _____

Part III: Short Answer/Listing
Provide brief answers to the following questions.

1. List five reasons why a family may decide to remodel their home. _____

_____

_____

_____

_____

2. What three basic factors should be considered before starting a remodeling project?_____

_____

_____

_____

3. List the five main types of remodeling. _____

_____

_____

_____

_____

_____

Name _____

4. List five remodel changes that can increase the efficiency of a kitchen. _____

_____

_____

_____

_____

5. List four improvements that are commonly made to bathrooms by remodeling. _____

_____

_____

_____

_____

6. Name four areas of the home that are generally not used as living space. _____

_____

_____

_____

_____

7. List three reasons why second story additions are much more expensive than ground-level
additions. _____

_____

_____

_____

8. Give an example of adaptive reuse. _____

_____

9. A good remodeling job requires three basic steps before any work begins. Name them. _____

_____

_____

_____

10. Name the three individuals that can help make a remodeling venture successful. _____

_____

_____

1.

Directions:
Prepare a remodel plan for this small house that includes the addition of a family/recreation room. The addition should be at least 12' × 14' in size. Scale the drawing for interior dimensions to maintain a relative scale to the existing floor plan.

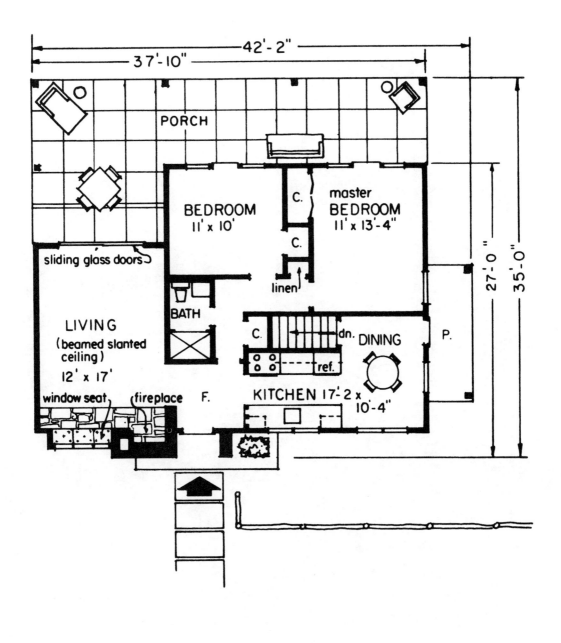

| REMODEL PLAN | NAME: | 37-1 |

Designing for Health and Safety

38

Text, Pages 715–738

Name _____

Course _____ Date _____ Score _____

Part I: Completion
Complete each sentence with the proper response. Place your answer on the space provided.

1. More injuries occur in the _____ than anywhere else.

1. _____

2. Statistics show that someone in the US is killed by _____ every two hours.

2. _____

3. Burning unseasoned wood in the fireplace or wood-burning stove will create a _____ buildup and lead to a chimney fire.

3. _____

4. There are two basic types of smoke detectors: ionization and _____.

4. _____

5. Carbon monoxide is produced from incomplete _____.

5. _____

6. _____ floods represent a high volume of fast-moving water that can appear suddenly.

6. _____

7. Some newer homes have a _____ room within the house that has been constructed to withstand tornado-force winds.

7. _____

8. Nine out of 10 hurricane fatalities can be attributed to a dome of ocean water called the storm _____.

8. _____

9. The hurricane season lasts from June through _____.

9. _____

10. _____ account for about one-third of the accidental deaths that occur in homes each year in the US.

10. _____

Part II: Short Answer/Listing
Provide brief answers to the following questions.

1. Name two of the leading causes of residential fires. _____

_____

_____

2. Name three locations where a smoke detector should be located in the home. _____

_____

_____

_____

3. Identify four symptoms of carbon monoxide poisoning. _____

_____

_____

4. Why are occupants generally not aware of a water vapor problem in their house? _____

_____

_____

5. Identify four health problems caused by indoor molds. _____

_____

_____

_____

6. What four structural elements of a house need to be strengthened to reduce damage from an earthquake? _____

_____

_____

_____

7. What is the minimum number of exits required for each occupied room in a residence?

_____

Part III: Multiple Choice
Select the best answer and write the corresponding letter in the space provided.

1. Class B extinguishers are used to extinguish fires involving _____.

   A. wood
   B. paper
   C. electrical devices
   D. grease

1. _____

2. The EPA has estimated that 1 out of _____ homes in the US has elevated levels of radon gas.

   A. 5
   B. 10
   C. 15
   D. 20

2. _____

3. Which type of mold is a greenish-black mold that can grow on material with a high cellulose and low nitrogen content?

   A. Cladosporium species.
   B. Pencillum species.
   C. Alternaria species.
   D. Stachybotrys atra.

3. _____

Name _____

4. Which of the following states or geographic areas is *not* located in an earthquake zone?

   A. Along the Mississippi River.
   B. The southern Appalachians.
   C. New England.
   D. The southern half of Texas.

4. _____

5. Which of the following has caused a greater loss of life and property than all other natural hazards?

   A. Floods.
   B. Tornadoes.
   C. Hurricanes.
   D. Earthquakes.

5. _____

6. The area of the country that runs north from Texas through eastern Nebraska and northeast to Indiana is called _____.

   A. a natural flood plain
   B. the New Madrid earthquake zone
   C. Hurricane Row
   D. Tornado Alley

6. _____

7. Records show that about _____ of all reported tornadoes have wind speeds of 112 mph or less.

   A. 65%
   B. 75%
   C. 85%
   D. 95%

7. _____

8. What three months are considered to be the tornado season in the US?

   A. January, February, and March.
   B. April, May, and June.
   C. July, August, and September.
   D. October, November, and December.

8. _____

9. New garage doors should be able to resist _____ mph winds.

   A. 100
   B. 110
   C. 120
   D. 130

9. _____

10. A tropical storm is considered a hurricane when winds have reached a constant speed of _____ miles per hour.

   A. 74
   B. 84
   C. 94
   D. 104

10. _____

Part IV: Problems/Activities

1.

Directions:
Match each of the health or safety concerns on the left with the common source, cause, or remedy on the right. Connect the matching descriptions with lines.

Typical accidents ☐
around the home

Structural fires ☐

Property damage from ☐
storm surge

Reduces blood's ability ☐
to transport oxygen

Flood damage ☐

Nose bleeds, sinusitis, ☐
chest congestion

"Sick house syndrome" ☐

Excessive humidity ☐
in the home

Radon ☐

Cannot extinguish a ☐
grease fire

Personal injury from ☐
a tornado

House damage from ☐
an earthquake

☐ Building in a flood plain

☐ Carbon monoxide poisoning

☐ Failure to meet building code
and use common sense

☐ Lack of ventilation

☐ Did not follow recommendations
of the CCCL

☐ Enters through cracks in the
walls and floors

☐ Falling asleep while smoking
and children with matches

☐ Exposure to harmful mold
in the house

☐ Sill and top plates not
bolted to the exterior walls

☐ Moisture and mold problems
in the home

☐ Using the wrong type of
fire extinguisher

☐ Failed to go to a safe
shelter

| HEALTH AND SAFETY | NAME: | 38-1 |

Career Opportunities

9

Text, Pages 739–748

Name _____

Course _____ Date _____ Score _____

Part I: Short Answer/Listing
Provide brief answers to the following questions.

1. Generally, what are the educational requirements to become an architect?_____
   _____

2. If you are artistic and have studied architectural drawing, which career choice might you
   pursue? _____
   _____

3. A college degree is generally required to be a specifications writer, however, how else might
   one become a specifications writer? _____
   _____

4. What knowledge/background should an estimator have?_____
   _____

5. List three reasons generally cited why new businesses fail._____
   _____
   _____

6. List five techniques that can be employed to sharpen concern for safety on the job. _____
   _____
   _____
   _____
   _____

7. In addition to job skills, what other important factor or trait do employers consider? _____
   _____

Part II: Completion

Complete each sentence with the proper response. Place your answer on the space provided.

1. One of the many responsibilities of the _____ is to check on the progress of the construction to see that the contractor is complying with the drawings and specifications.

1. _____

2. According to OSHA, _____ is one of the most dangerous occupations in the United States.

2. _____

3. The selling price of a structure is generally based on the information prepared by a(n) _____.

3. _____

4. Grade level, property lines, and site description are based on the work of a(n) _____.

4. _____

5. For a teaching career at the high school level, you should pursue a _____ degree in construction or industrial technology.

5. _____

6. Purchasing, estimating and bidding, quality control, and site supervision are just a few areas of specialization of a(n) _____.

6. _____

Part III: Multiple Choice

Select the best answer and write the corresponding letter in the space provided.

1. What is the primary function of an architect?

   A. Make copies of original drawings.
   B. Design structures that meet the standards for health, safety, and property.
   C. Make renderings and presentations.
   D. None of the above.

1. _____

2. To become an architectural drafter, you should have completed high school, possess a knowledge of architectural drawing, and:

   A. Be familiar with a CADD system.
   B. Have an art background.
   C. Possess an understanding of economics.
   D. All of the above.

2. _____

3. A specifications writer should have a knowledge of:

   A. Construction, building materials, and surveying.
   B. Building materials, hardware, and art.
   C. Hardware, construction, and building materials.
   D. All of the above.

3. _____

4. Responsibilities of the surveyor include:

   A. Preparing plats and maps of features above and below ground level.
   B. Preparing descriptions of property.
   C. Planning and subdividing property.
   D. All of the above.

4. _____

Name _____

Part IV: Matching

Match the correct term with its description listed below. Place the corresponding letter on the space provided.

A. Architect
B. Architectural drafter
C. Construction technologist
D. Estimator

E. Residential designer
F. Specifications writer
G. Surveyor

1. A professional who creates a design based on a client's requirements.

1. _____

2. Draws the details of working drawings.

2. _____

3. Prepares a description of materials, methods, and fixtures to be used in construction.

3. _____

4. Calculates cost of materials and labor.

4. _____

5. Establishes areas and boundaries of real estate property.

5. _____

6. Requires knowledge in science and construction methods.

6. _____

7. Represented by the American Institute of Building and Design.

7. _____

1.

Directions:
Present a brief summary of the duties and educational requirements of each of the jobs/positions listed on these two pages.

Architect—

Architectural Drafter—

Architectural Illustrator—

Specifications Writer—

(continued)

CAREERS	NAME:	39-1

Estimator—

Surveyor—

Construction Technologist—

Teacher of Architectural Drafting—